P9-BYA-829

Aristophanes

Acharnians

2/21

The Focus Classical Library
Series Editors • James Clauss and Michael Halleran

Aristophanes

Acharnians

**Translated with
Introduction and Notes**

Jeffrey Henderson

Focus Classical Library
Focus Publishing/R. Pullins Company
Newburyport, MA 01950

Copyright © 2003 Jeffrey Henderson

ISBN 1-58510-087-0

Cover: Hydria from Louvre, Paris. Used with permission.

This book is published by Focus Publishing/R Pullins Company, PO Box 369, Newburyport MA 01950 All rights are reserved. No part of this publication may be reproduced, stored in a retrieval system, produced on stage or otherwise performed, transmitted by any means, electronic, mechanical, by photocopying, recording, or by any other media or means without the prior written permission of the publisher.

Printed in the United States of America
10 9 8 7 6 5 4 3 2 1

Contents

For Pat, Alex, and Andreas

Preface

Acharnians, first performed in 425 BC, is a comedy about the ordinary farmer Dicaeopolis, evacuated from his land and pressed into service in the Peloponnesian War. Failing to interest his fellow Athenians in seeking peace, he arranges a magical private peace for himself. On the way back to the good life in the countryside, he is confronted by a crowd of patriotic charcoal-burners from Acharnae who want to stone him as a traitor. But by restaging himself as a tragic hero, Dicaeopolis convinces the Acharnians of the justice of his actions and proceeds to expose the corruption of the politicians and generals, especially General Lamachus. After establishing his own free-trade zone and collecting food for a sumptuous banquet, Dicaeopolis wins the national drinking contest, while General Lamachus suffers from ignominious wounds.

Acharnians is both a hilarious comedy and a forceful indictment of war. Today it is just as entertaining as theater, and just as relevant as a view of the best and worst of Western civilization, as it was over two millennia ago. In its mirror modern people can catch a glimpse of where we came from, where our best ideals have aimed us, and how far we have come (or not come) thus far.

This is a translation of *Acharnians* into contemporary American verse, designed for both readers and performers, and presupposing no knowledge of classical Greece or classical Greek theater. I render the Greek text line by line so as to give the sense of its original scope and pace, using for the dialogue and songs verse-forms that are familiar to modern audiences. Where the original text refers to people, places, things and events whose significance modern audiences cannot reasonably be expected to know or to infer from the text, and which are inessential to its main themes, I have tried to find easily comprehensible alternatives that preserve the import of the original. What may be unfamiliar in the text is discussed in footnotes.

The conventions of Aristophanic comedy included the frank portrayal and discussion of religion, politics and sex (including nudity and obscenity). In *Acharnians* all three are brilliantly intertwined. I have reproduced this feature as accurately as possible within my general guideline of easy intelligibility. To do otherwise would be to falsify the play. These three areas are of fundamental importance to any society; one of Aristophanes' chief aims was to make humor of them while at the same time encouraging his audience to think about them in ways discouraged, or even forbidden, outside the comic theater. The issue of freedom of speech is especially relevant to *Acharnians*, for it was an anti-war play produced in a time of war by a poet whom a powerful politician had recently tried to persecute into silence. For those made uncomfortable by such provocative theater, *Acharnians* provides an opportunity to ask themselves why.

The Introduction contains sections on Aristophanes and the genre of Attic Old Comedy which his plays represent; Acharnians and the historical situation to which it was originally addressed; conventions of ancient production and suggestions for modern performers; and suggestions for further reading. Like the translation and notes, the Introduction requires no previous expertise, and so is suitable for readers and students making their first acquaintance with Aristophanes.

The translation is based on the Greek text by Alan H. Sommerstein (Warminster 1980).

For suggestions and helpful criticisms I am grateful to Donald McGuire and Amy Richlin.

Boston   JJH
May 1992

Greece and Environs

Introduction

Aristophanes and Old Comedy

Aristophanes of Athens, the earliest comic playwright from whom whole works survive, was judged in antiquity to be the foremost poet of Old Attic Comedy, a theatrical genre of which he was one of the last practitioners and of which his eleven surviving plays are our only complete examples. His plays are valued principally for the exuberance of their wit and fantasy, for the purity and elegance of their language, and for the light they throw on the domestic and political life of Athens in an important era of its history. Legend has it that when the Syracusan tyrant Dionysius wanted to inform himself about 'the republic of the Athenians,' Plato sent him the plays of Aristophanes.

Little is known about Aristophanes' life apart from his theatrical career. He was born *ca.* 447/6, the son of one Philippus of the urban deme Cydathenaeum and the tribe Pandionis, and he died probably between 386 and 380. By his twenties his hair had thinned or receded enough that his rivals could call him bald. He seems to have had land-holdings on, or some other connection with, the island of Aegina, a connection that detractors and enemies exploited early in his career in an attempt to call his Athenian citizenship into question. He was twice prosecuted by a fellow demesman, the popular politician Cleon, for the political impropriety of two of his plays (*Babylonians* and *Knights*), but he was not convicted. Early in the fourth century he represented his tribe in the prestigious government position of Councillor. Four comic poets of the fourth century, Araros, Philetaerus, Philippus and Nicostratus, are reputed in ancient sources to be his sons.

In the dialogue *Symposium* Plato portrays Aristophanes as being at home among the social and intellectual elite of Athens. Although the historical truth of Plato's portrayal is uncertain, Aristophanes' plays do generally espouse the social, moral and political sentiments of contemporary upper-class conservatives: nostalgia for the good old days of the early democracy, which defeated the Persians and built the empire; dismay at the decadence, corruption and political divisiveness of his own day; hostility toward the new breed of popular leaders who emerged after the death of the aristocratic

1

Perikles in 429; impatience with the leadership and slow progress of the Peloponnesian War (431-404); unhappiness about current artistic and intellectual trends. There is no question that Aristophanes' comic expression of such views reflected, and to a degree shaped, community opinion, and that comedy could occasionally have a distinct political impact. But the fact that Aristophanes emerged politically and artistically unscathed from the war, from two oligarchic revolutions (411 and 404), and from two democratic restorations (411 and 403) suggests that on the whole his role in Athenian politics was more satirical, moral(istic) and poetical than practical; and the perennial popularity of his plays would seem to indicate that the sentiments they express were broadly shared among the theatrical public.

The period of Old Comedy at Athens began in 486 BC, when comedy first became part of the festival of the Greater Dionysia; by convention it ended in 388 BC, when Aristophanes produced his last play. During this period some 600 comedies were produced. We know the titles of some fifty comic poets and the titles of some 300 plays. We have eleven complete plays by Aristophanes, the first one dating from 425, and several thousand fragments of other plays by Aristophanes and other poets, most of them only a line or so long and very few deriving from plays written before 440.

The principal occasions for the production of comedies were the Greater Dionysia, held in late March or early April, and (from 440) the Lenaea, held in late January or early February. These were national festivals honoring the wine-god Dionysus, whose cult from very early times had included mimetic features. The theatrical productions that were the highlight of the festivals were competitions in which poets, dancers, actors, producers and musicians competed for prizes that were awarded by judges at the close of the festival. The Greater Dionysia was held in the Theater of Dionysus on the south slope of the Acropolis, which accommodated some 17,000 spectators, including both Athenian and foreign visitors. The Lenaea, which only Athenians attended, was held elsewhere in the city (we do not know where). By the fourth century the Lenaea was held in the Theater of Dionysus also, but it is unclear when the relocation occurred.

At these festivals comedy shared the theater with tragedy and satyr-drama, genres that had been produced at the Greater Dionysia since the sixth century. The first "city" contest in tragedy is dated to 534, when the victorious actor-poet was Thespis, from whose name actors are still called thespians. But it is not certain that Thespis' contest was held at the Greater Dionysia, and in any case this festival seems to have experienced major changes after the overthrow of the tyranny and the establishment of democracy, that is, after the reforms of Cleisthenes in 508. Tragedy dramatized stories from heroic myth, emphasizing dire personal and social events that had befallen hero(in)es and their families in the distant past, and mostly in places other than Athens. By convention, the poetry and music of tragedy were highly stylized and archaic. Satyr-drama, which was composed by the same poets who wrote tragedy, had similar conventions, except that the heroic stories were treated in a humorous fashion and the chorus was composed of satyrs: mischievous followers of Dionysus who were part human and part animal.

Comedy, by contrast, had different conventions of performance (see III, below) and was less restricted by conventions of language, music and subject. That is probably why the composers and performers of tragedy and satyr-drama were never the same ones who composed and performed comedy. The language of comedy was basically colloquial, though it often parodies the conventions of other (particularly tragic) poetry, and was free to include indecent, even obscene material. The music and dancing, too, tended to reflect popular styles. The favorite subjects of comedy were free-form mythological burlesque; domestic situations featuring everyday character types; and political satire portraying people and events of current interest in the public life of the Athenians. Our eleven surviving comedies all fall into this last category. Mythological and domestic comedy continued to flourish after the Old Comic period, but political comedy seems to have died out: a casualty not merely of changing theatrical tastes but also of the social and political changes that followed the Athenians' loss of the Peloponnesian War, and with it their empire, in 404. To understand the significance of political comedy, we must look first at the political system of which it was an organic feature: the phase of radical democracy inaugurated by the reforms of Ephialtes in 462/1 and lasting until the end of the century.

Democracy means 'rule of the demos' (sovereign people). In fifth-century Athens democracy was radical in that the sovereignty of the demos was more absolute than in any other society before or since. The demos consisted of all citizen males at least eighteen years of age. All decisions affecting the governance and welfare of the state were made by the direct and unappealable vote of the demos. The state was managed by members of the demos at least thirty years of age, who were chosen by lot from a list of eligible citizens and who held office in periods ranging from one day to one year. The only exceptions were military commanders, who were elected to one-year terms, and holders of certain ancient priesthoods, who inherited their positions. The demos determined by vote whether or not anyone holding any public position was qualified to do his job, and after completion of his term, whether he had done it satisfactorily. All military commanders, and most holders of powerful allotted offices, came from the wealthy classes, but their success depended on the good will of the demos as a whole.

One of the most important allotted offices in the democracy was that of choregus, sponsor of a chorus. Choregi were allotted from a list of men wealthy enough to hold this office, for they had to recruit and pay for the training, costuming and room and board of the chorus that would perform at one of the festivals. In the case of a comic chorus this involved 24 dancers and the musicians who would accompany them. Being choregus gave a man an opportunity to display his wealth and refinement for the benefit of the demos as a whole and to win a prize that would confer prestige on himself and his dancers. Some wealthy men therefore volunteered to be a choregus instead of waiting for their names to be drawn. On the other hand, a man who put on a cheap or otherwise unsatisfactory chorus could expect to suffer a significant loss of public prestige.

All other festival expenses, including stipends for the poet and his actors and for prizes, were undertaken by vote of the demos and paid for from public funds. A poet got a place in the festival by submitting a draft some six months in advance to the office-holder in charge of the festival. Ancient sources say that at least the choral parts of the proposed play had to be submitted. How much more was submitted we do not know. But revision up to the day of the performance was certainly possible, since many allusions in comedy refer to events occurring very shortly before the festival: most notably the death of Sophocles shortly before the performance of *Frogs* in 405.

If he got on the program, the poet would be given his stipend and assigned his actors. He and the choregus would then set about getting the performance ready for the big day, the poet acting as music master, choreographer and director, the choregus rounding up, and paying the expenses of, the best dancers he could find. While tragic poets produced three tragedies and a satyr-drama, comic poets produced only one comedy.

Thus comedy, as a theatrical spectacle, was an organic feature of Athenian democracy. But its poetic, musical and mimetic traditions were much older, deriving from forms of entertainment developed by cultivated members of the aristocratic families that had governed Attica before the democracy. One such traditional form was the komos (band of revellers), which gave comedy (komoidia: 'song of the komos') its name. A komos was made up of some solidary group (a military, religious or family group, for example), often in masks or costumes, which entertained onlookers on many kinds of festive and religious occasions.

Part of the entertainment was abuse and criticism of individuals or groups standing outside the solidarity of the komos. The victims might be among the onlookers or they might be members of a rival komos. The komos sang and danced as a group, and its leader (who was no doubt also the poet) could speak by himself to his komos, to the onlookers or to a rival komos-leader. No doubt at a very early stage the komos was a competitive entertainment by which a given group could, in artistic ways, make those claims and criticisms against rival groups which at other times they might make in more overtly political ways. The targets of komastic abuse were often the village's most powerful men and groups. Thus the tradition of the komos was useful in allowing the expression of personal and political hostilities which would otherwise have been difficult to express safely: the misbehavior of powerful individuals, disruptive but unactionable gossip, the shortcomings of citizens in groups or as a whole. Here komos served a cathartic function, as a kind of social safety valve, allowing a relatively harmless airing of tensions before they could become dangerous, and also as a means of social communication and social control, upholding generally held norms and calling attention to derelictions.

But in addition to its critical and satiric aspects, komos (like all festive activities) had an idealistic side, helping people to envision the community as it would be if everyone agreed on norms and lived up to them, and a utopian side as well, allowing people to imagine how wonderful life would be if reality were as human beings, especially ordinary human beings, would like it to be. In this function komos provided a time-out from the cares and burdens of everyday life.

Old Comedies were theatrical versions of komos: the band of dancers with their leader was now a comic chorus involved in a story enacted by actors on a stage. The chorus still resembled a komos in two ways: (1) as performers, it competed against rival choruses, and (2) in its dramatic identity it represented, at least initially, a distinct group or groups: in *Clouds*, for example, it initially represents the guiding spirits of Socrates' Thinkery. The comic chorus differs from a komos in that at a certain point in the play it drops its dramatic identity and thereafter represents the festival's traditional comic chorus, which reflects the celebrating community as a whole. At this point, its leader steps forward, on behalf of the poet, to advise and admonish the spectators, and his chorus might sing abusive songs about particular individuals in the audience.

The actors in the stage-area had been amalgamated with the chorus during the sixth century. Their characteristic costumes (III, below) and antics were depicted in vase-paintings of that period in many parts of Greece, suggesting a much older tradition of comic mimesis. As early as the Homeric period (8th and 7th centuries) we find mythological burlesque and such proto-comedy as the Thersites-episode in the second book of the *Iliad*. In this period, too, the iambic poets flourished. Named for the characteristic rhythm of their verses, which also became the characteristic rhythm of actors in Athenian drama, the iambic poets specialized in self-revelation, popular story-telling, earthy gossip, and personal enmities, often creating fictitious first-person identities and perhaps also using masks and disguise. They were credited with pioneering poetic styles invective, obscenity and colloquialism.

The characters on the Old Comic stage preserved many of these traditions, but like the chorus they were an adaptation to the democratic festivals, most notably in political comedy. In Aristophanes' plays, the world depicted by the plot and the characters on stage was the world of the spectators in their civic roles: as heads of families and participants in governing the democratic state. We see the demos in its various capacities; the competitors for public influence; the men who hold or seek offices; the social, intellectual and artistic celebrities. We hear formal debate on current issues, including its characteristic invective. We get a decision, complete with winners and losers, and we see the outcome. This depiction of public life was designed both to arouse laughter and to encourage reflection about people and events in ways not possible in other public contexts. Thus it was at once a distorted and an accurate depiction of public life, somewhat like a modern political cartoon.

Aristophanic comedies typically depict Athens in the grip of a terrible and intractable problem (e.g. the war, bad political leaders, an unjust jury-system, dangerous artistic or intellectual trends), which is solved in a fantastic but essentially plausible way, often by a comic hero. The characters of these heroic plays fall into two main categories, sympathetic and unsympathetic. The sympathetic ones (the hero and his/her supporters), are fictitious creations embodying ideal civic types or representing ordinary Athenians. The unsympathetic ones embody disapproved civic behavior and usually represent specific leaders or categories of leaders. The sympathetic characters advocate positions held by political or social minorities and are therefore 'outsiders.' But they are shown winning out against the unsympathetic ones, who represent the current status quo. Characters or chorus-members representing the demos as a whole are portrayed as initially sceptical or hostile to the sympathetic character(s), but in the end they are persuaded; those responsible for the problem are disgraced or expelled; and Athens is recalled to a sense of her true (traditional) ideals and is thus renewed. In the (thoroughly democratic) comic view, the people are never at fault for their problems, but are merely good people who have been deceived by bad leaders. Thus the comic poets tried to persuade the actual demos (the spectators) to change its mind about issues that had been decided but might be changed (the war, as in *Acharnians* and *Lysistrata*), or to discard dangerous novelties as in *Clouds*). Aristophanes at least once succeeded: after the performance of *Frogs* he was awarded a crown by the city for the advice that was given by the chorus-leader in that play and that was subsequently adopted by the demos.

In this way, the institution of Old Comedy performed functions essential to any democracy: public airing of minority views and criticism of those holding power. In this function, the Old Comic festivals were organized protest by ordinary people against its advisers and leaders. But they were also an opportunity to articulate civic ideals: one identified the shortcomings of the status quo by holding it up against a vision of things as they ought to (or used to) be. The use of satire and criticism within a plot addressing itself to important issues of national scope was thus a democratic adaptation of such pre-democratic traditions as komos and iambic poetry. That the comic festivals were state-run and not privately organized, a partnership between the elite and the masses, is striking evidence of the openness and self-confidence of a full democracy: the demos was completely in charge, so it did not fear attacks on its celebrities or resent admonition by the poets. In particular, the Athenians were much less inclined than we are to treat their political leaders with fear and reverence: since the Athenian people were themselves the government, they tended to see their leaders more as advisors and competitors for public stature that august representatives of the state. And even comic poets enjoyed the traditional role of Greek poets and orators generally: to admonish, criticise and advise on behalf of the people. In Socrates' case, the demos seems to have taken Aristophanes' criticisms to heart, however exaggerated they may have been: as Plato reported in his *Apology*, the *Clouds'* 'nonsensical' portrait of Socrates was a factor in the people's decision, 24 years later, to condemn him to death.

The comic poets did not, however, enjoy a complete license to say anything they pleased: were that the case they could not have expected anyone to take what they had to say seriously. Following each festival there was an assembly in which anyone who had a legal complaint could come forward. Although the Athenians recognized freedom of speech, they did not tolerate any speech whatever. No one who spoke in public, comic poets included, could criticize the democratic constitution and the inherent rightness of the demos' rule, or say anything else that might in some way harm the democracy or compromise the integrity of the state religion. And abuse of individuals could not be slanderous. But the Athenian definition of slander differed from ours. Our slander laws are designed to protect individuals, whereas the Athenian slander laws were designed to protect the institutions of the democracy: they forbade malicious and unfounded abuse of individuals if and only if the abuse might compromise a man's civic standing or eligibility to participate in the democracy, for example, accusations that would, if taken seriously, make a man ineligible to participate in public life. And so, if the criticism and abuse we find in Old Comedy often seems outrageous by our standards, it is because we differ from the fifth-century Athenians in our definition of outrageous, not because comic poets were held to no standards.

Aristophanes, for example, was twice sued by the politician Cleon, once for slandering the demos and its officers in front of visiting foreigners (in *Babylonians* of 426) and once for slandering him (in *Knights* of 424). In the first instance the demos decided not to hear the case. In the second the poet and the politician settled out of court (in his play *Wasps* Aristophanes subsequently boasted that he had not abided by the agreement). The demos could also enact new laws restricting comic freedoms, to protect the integrity of the military or legal systems. One of these laws was enacted in 440, when Athens went to war against her own ally Samos; another, enacted in 415, forbade mention by name in comedy of any of the men who had recently been implicated in the parody of the Eleusinian Mysteries of Demeter. Possibly the demos wanted to protect from public innuendo those who might be suspected, but might not ultimately be convicted, of this crime: as we have seen, such innuendo would fall within the legal definition of slander. And possibly the demos did not want to take the chance that a comic poet might speak sympathetically of the profaners, as they often spoke for other underdogs; it is perhaps relevant that three of the men condemned seem to have been comic poets.

Acharnians: Comic Hero, Comic Poet and Society

Acharnians is a comedy about the ordinary farmer Dicaeopolis, evacuated from his land and pressed into service in the Peloponnesian War. Failing to interest his fellow Athenians in seeking peace, he arranges a magical private peace for himself. On the way back to the good life in the countryside, he is confronted by a crowd of patriotic charcoal-burners from Acharnae who want to stone him as a traitor. But by restaging himself as a tragic hero, Dicaeopolis convinces the Acharnians of the justice of his actions and proceeds to expose the corruption of the politicians and generals, especially General Lamachus. After establishing his own free-trade zone and collecting food for a sumptuous banquet, Dicaeopolis wins the national drinking contest, while General Lamachus suffers from ignominious wounds.

Acharnians was Aristophanes' third (and first extant) play, produced at the Lenaea festival in 425, and it won the first prize for comedy. Its plot is characteristic of Aristophanes' heroic plays (the others are *Peace*, *Birds*, *Lysistrata*, and *Assemblywomen*). By means of a fantastic scheme a hero(ine), who represents a class of citizens who feel frustrated or victimized by the operations of contemporary society, manages to evade or alter the situation of which (s)he initially complains and proceeds to effect a triumph of wish-fulfillment over reality. Those powers human, natural or divine which would obstruct the scheme are either converted by argument or overcome by guile, magic or force. At the end there is a restoration of normality (typically portrayed in terms of an idealized civic past) and a celebration (typically portrayed in terms of food, wine and sex). The celebration is reserved for the hero(ine) and the hero(ine)'s supporters, for the initial obstructors and those who would undeservedly benefit by the hero(ine)'s success have been expelled or disgraced.

Although the hero(ine) typically represents the views of a social or political minority, and the scheme bypasses or undermines the powers currently enforcing the status quo, the hero(ine)'s goal is one likely to be shared by most spectators when in an idealistic mood, and the arguments (s)he uses to defend it are designed to appeal to their interests and sense of justice. The powers are portrayed entirely without sympathy as self-interested, corrupt and misguided, and the status quo as unnecessarily burdensome for ordinary, decent people. The status quo is shown to be as it is because ordinary people have been deceived by their leaders. Once the leaders are exposed, the hero(ine) can resume the comfortable and just life that (in comic myth) had existed before troublemakers disrupted it.

In this utopian scenario, the harsh and intractable realities of life, politics and international aggression are comically transformed so that an ordinary farmer can arrange a separate peace, discredit powerful politicians and generals, and alone enjoy the blessings of peace. The transformation seems quite plausible because Aristophanes appeals to the wishes of the spectators for a better world, the world as it presumably was before the war, where all would be happy and prosperous and where there would be no more violence. He also appeals to the feeling of the average citizens that their wishes would be more likely to come true were there no authorities in the way, constantly reminding them of unpleasant duties. After all, the god Dionysos, patron of the theatrical festivals, was emblematic of peace and freedom. This combination of regressive wish-fulfillment and oedipal rebellion allowed a communal release of tensions. Insofar as their release was motivated by acceptable civic ideals (peace and fairness) and achieved in humorous fantasy, it was safe: cohesive not disruptive. But insofar as it was a valid expression of people's real war-weariness, an expression of social discontent running beneath the surface of official public discourse, it was also fair warning to the people's leaders that public patience might not last indefinitely.

Like Aristophanes' preceding two plays, *Acharnians* was produced not by the poet himself, but by his friend Callistratus; not until the following year was the young poet (then in his early 20's) confident enough to produce plays on his own. But that does not mean that Callistratus was thought to be the author: entrusting production to others, as is the rule today, was not unusual in Aristophanes' day either, and Aristophanes would for various reasons occasionally do so throughout his career; moreover, in *Knights* 512-13 Aristophanes says that many people had for a long time been asking him why he had not yet produced one of his own plays. The issue of authorship is important in the case of *Acharnians* because of the play's unusual identification of its hero with the poet himself. In order to understand this identification, we must review the contemporary Athenian situation and Aristophanes' stance toward it, which had become a public issue.

Since 431 Athens and Sparta had been fighting what is now called the Peloponnesian War, a war that involved nearly all Greeks and even the Persian Empire. The principal issue was the Athenians' growing imperial power. The alliance of Aegean states that had begun fifty years earlier as the Delian League, a panhellenic defensive alliance against future Persian invasions, had gradually been changed into a collection of tribute-paying allies subject to Athens. As a result Athens had become dominant at sea, very wealthy and aggressively expansionist. In addition, Athens used her empire to spread democracy at the expense of traditional ruling elites, sometimes by force. Sparta and her allies (the "Peloponnesians") considered democracy to be a dangerous idea and the Athenians to be imperial tyrants (a label that the Athenians did not wholly reject); Athenian strength, if unchecked, dangerously threatened the balance of power in the Greek world.

In 431 Pericles, Athens' leading general and statesman, convinced his countrymen to resist Peloponnesian demands that Athens abandon such aggressive policies as the economic blockade of Megara. He predicted that, if war was the result, Athenian wealth and naval power would quickly force the Peloponnesians to abandon their resistance and acquiesce to Athenian dominance. But his plan required that the Athenians not oppose the Spartans on land, where they were superior, so that the Attic countryside would have to be evacuated and its residents moved into fortified Athens for the duration. That meant extremely uncomfortable quarters for those without relatives or friends in the city. Thucydides (2.16) describes the reaction of the rural population of whom this sacrifice was asked:

> For the better part of their history the Athenians had lived in independent country settlements. Even after the political unification of Attica, most Athenians, both in earlier generations and down to the time of this present war being born and raised in the country, retained their traditional rural character. So it was not easy for them to have to move with their entire households, especially since they had only recently re-established themselves after the Persian invasions. They felt oppressed and resentful at having to abandon their homes and their temples, venerable symbols of a patriotic past, and at having to change their whole way of life, each leaving behind what he regarded as his own polis.

In spite of these hardships, however, the rural Athenians supported the war: like all Athenians, they benefited from the empire and would do their part to resist Spartan interference.

But by 425 it was clear that Pericles had overestimated Athenian superiority and underestimated the determination of the Peloponnesians; and there had been additional unforeseen difficulties. Most serious was the terrible plague that decimated the Athenians in 429 and would continue to break out, on and off, for the next five years; Pericles was one of its victims. By 428 the war-fund had run out, requiring the Athenians to levy emergency taxes and to raise the tribute quotas. Some members of the empire had begun to revolt or to contemplate revolt, thus requiring the Athenians to divert valuable energy policing their own allies. After six years of fighting, the Athenians had won important victories, but so had the enemy. No one could say when victory could be expected, or even how it was to be defined.

These conditions produced political unrest. In particular, the devastation of the Attic countryside and the suffering of the evacuees was very demoralizing. Many had begun to question the rationale for continued fighting and to consider whether a negotiated settlement might not be preferable.

But such views were still opposed by the majority, including the majority of evacuees, whose initial support of the war had indeed been fortified by a determination to get revenge on the Peloponnesians whatever the cost. The policy of continued war was championed and guided by Cleon, who had replaced Pericles as the leading politician of Athens. Cleon, a forceful orator and the first great populist (enemies said "demagogue"), strove to maintain unity and morale behind the war effort, to assure adequate finances and to enforce efficient civic, imperial and military administration. He ruthlessly attacked as unpatriotic, even treasonous, anyone he thought was undermining these goals: Athenian or allied rebels, dissidents, malingerers, hoarders, black-marketeers, Spartan sympathizers, advocates of negotiated peace.

Aristophanes himself was one of those attacked. After *Babylonians* (produced in 426), in which Aristophanes had criticized Athenian imperial rule and perhaps also the war, Cleon denounced him before the Council for having slandered the magistrates, Councillors and Athenian people before an audience that included foreign allies. He also seems to have called Aristophanes's Athenian birth (and therefore his citizenship) into question by citing the poet's ties to Aegina. Evidently the Council did not refer the charges to the Assembly or to a court for trial, but dismissed them. Nevertheless, Aristophanes thought that Cleon's attack had to be answered. In *Acharnians*, Aristophanes frontally challenges the rationale for the war and the motives of its political and military advocates, and defends both his own patriotism and the value to democracy of free comic expression.

The hero, Dicaeopolis ("Just City"), represents the displaced countrymen, who have sacrificed most for the war, and the common soldiers, who do the actual fighting. Tired of combat and the discomforts of urban life, he longs to return to his rural deme (local community) to resume the happy peacetime life that has been disrupted by the war. He has repeatedly gone to the Assembly to raise the issue of negotiations, but his effort is wasted. Dicaeopolis's fellow Athenians want only to gape at the politicians, ambassadors and their barbarian allies and mercenaries; no one has the least interest in talking about peace. Dicaeopolis himself is ruled out of order and roughed up by barbarians, while his fellow citizens turn a deaf ear to his cries.

At this point Dicaeopolis decides on a radical solution. With the help of a magical friend, he acquires a 30-year peace for himself and his family, which takes the form of bottle of 30-year-old wine. This peace enables Dicaeopolis to return to the country, where he will be able to live on his own produce, trade with whomever he likes (even enemy states), drink his own wine at the local festivals and resume a life of ease and sexual gratification. He and his family celebrate by holding the festival of the Rural Dionysia.

But Dicaeopolis is soon confronted by a Chorus of outraged old men: veterans of the glorious Athenian struggle against the Persians, builders of the empire and supporters of the war. They are charcoal-burners from the deme Acharnae, the largest rural deme and one that had from the beginning of the war been especially hard-hit by Spartan incursions. The Acharnians as a result were perhaps the most fiercely pro-war and anti-Spartan of all Athenians, and they intend to stone Dicaeopolis to death as a traitor even before they hear what he has to say in his own defense. But by taking a coal-scuttle hostage, Dicaeopolis secures a hearing and bets his life on his ability to convince the Acharnians (and beyond them, the spectators) of the justice of his separate peace.

At this critical juncture the forward motion of the plot suddenly stops and the action onstage becomes invisible to the chorus. Dicaeopolis announces that, before he makes his speech, he must first go to the house of the tragic poet, Euripides, to borrow pitiful garb and persuasive eloquence. The audience, he says, will know him for who he truly is, while the Acharnians will be deceived. The scene with Euripides, where Dicaeopolis rummages through the tragedian's stock of costumes and props and reconstitutes himself as the tragic hero, Telephus, is a splendid example of metatheater (dramatist and performers calling attention to their own theatrical artifices), by which Aristophanes locates his play within comedy's wider theatrical and political contexts.

The myth of Telephus had most recently been dramatized by Euripides in 438. Although only fragments of the play survive, its main outlines are clear. Although he was the son of the great Greek hero Heracles and Auge, daughter of King Aleus of Arcadia, Telephus had become king of barbarian Mysia, a kingdom south of Troy. When the Greek expedition against Troy mistakenly attacked Mysia, Telephus was wounded by Achilles. When an oracle told him that his wound could be healed only by its inflictor, Telephus went to Argos, disguised as a Mysian beggar, to look for Achilles. In a speech, he defended himself and the Mysians by arguing that the Greeks would have acted the same way if they had suffered an unprovoked attack. He probably also questioned the Greeks' motive for the Trojan War (the abduction of Helen) and urged the Greeks to look at matters from a Trojan perspective. When Telephus' disguise was exposed and he was threatened with death, he took refuge at an altar, with the baby Orestes as hostage, and convinced the Greeks that he, too, was in fact a Greek. Achilles then agreed to provide a cure for his wound, and as the result of another oracle Telephus agreed to guide the Greeks to Troy.

Dicaeopolis adopts Telephus' strategems of hostage-taking and disguise and adapts elements of Telephus' speech of self-defence to his own situation. He tells the Acharnians that he has just as much reason to hate the Spartans as they do, but that they are wrong to blame everything on the Spartans, for it was certain Athenians who actually started the trouble. First, base-born informers profited by denouncing Megarian goods; then drunken young gamblers stole a Megarian whore. When the Megarians retaliated by stealing two whores from Pericles' mistress, Aspasia, Pericles turned all Greece upside-down in his wrath. Thus the Spartans had good reason to fight and the Athenians ought to re-examine their own reasons for continuing the war.

It is to be noted that, while Dicaeopolis offers reasons for his decision to make a separate peace, he does not defend the separate peace itself, nor does he ever suggest that anyone else follow his lead. Indeed, he refuses to share his peace with any of those who ask, with the sole exception of a bride (since women had no part in bringing on the war). Dicaeopolis's exposure of the war's inadequate motivation, its self-interested military and political leaders and its lack of rewards for everybody else—at best these arguments make his separate peace seem more understandable and more palatable; most people would agree that there was some truth to them. But however plausible Dicaeopolis's motivation may be, and however enviable his subsequent happiness, Aristophanes evidently had no wish directly to advocate desertion in time of war.

While the embattled Dicaeopolis impersonates Telephus in addressing the Chorus, he simultaneously represents the embattled Aristophanes in addressing the spectators: like Telephus, Aristophanes has been slandered and attacked because of a successful and justified previous attack on his countrymen (the criticisms he had made in Babylonians):

> Do not be angry, you men who watch the play,
> if, though a beggar, I speak before Athenians
> of state affairs while making comedy.
> For comedy too concerns itself with justice,
> and what I will say will shock you but be just.
> And this time Cleon won't make allegations
> that I slander the polis in front of foreigners;
> for we are alone, it's a Lenaean competition,
> the foreigners aren't yet here, nor tribute-money
> nor allied troops from the cities of our empire,
> but now we are by ourselves. (497-507)

Later, in the play's Parabasis (629 n.), Aristophanes further adapts the Telephean defense. He claims that he deserves no anger but praise from the Athenians for having opened their eyes to the flatteries, deceptions, self-interest and general mismanagement of the empire (and also the war?) by Cleon and the other leading politicians. Now the allies gladly come with their tribute, eager to see the poet who alone had the courage to tell the truth, and the King of Persia has told the Spartans that they cannot prevail over a city that has such a poet for its adviser. That is why the Spartans are eager for peace, and as for their demand for Aegina, they want it not for strategic reasons but to get this poet for themselves. For he alone talks justice and truth, and so selflessly and courageously champions the best interests of his people. Like Telephus, Aristophanes is discovered to be a true compatriot, his criticisms are justified, and he will lead his countrymen on to a just victory.

In so adapting Euripides' hero to his own purposes, Aristophanes used a technique, which he himself pioneered, called paratragedy: the usurpation of tragic style and elevation as vehicles to express comic ideas. (Paratragedy may thus be distinguished from parody of tragedy, which merely reproduces tragic style in order to deflate it.) By means of paratragedy Aristophanes could exploit the strengths of each genre. Tragedy could examine social and political problems with great pathos and intensity, but only through the veil of heroic myth, to whose distant world it restricted itself. Comedy was free to deal with such problems topically and directly, with unmediated reference to the spectators and their world, but only in a humorous fashion, since pathos and intensity were alien to the comic mode. As the Assembly scene that opens the play seems to suggest, comedy by itself, like Dicaeopolis by himself, was unable to muster the pathos and intensity needed to persuade the Athenians. Some way had to be found to intensify the comic appeal. Paratragedy was the answer: if the Athenians took Telephus so seriously, would they not listen more seriously to his paratragic counterpart?

Through the paratragic "borrowing" of Telephus from Euripides, Aristophanes creates a play within a play and a complex layering of dramatic disguises. He also, metatheatrically, calls attention to what he is doing as poet and playwright, thus educating the spectators about the role of theatrical illusion and persuasion. Dicaeopolis manages to deceive, and thus to persuade, the Chorus by means of his beggar's disguise, like Telephus before the Greeks. But the spectators have already been shown, in the dressing-scene with Euripides, what to expect and are thus taught to see through the disguise. Behind the beggar is the comic-as-tragic hero, just as behind him is the comic-as-tragic poet: as Dicaeopolis is comically threatened in the play for his courageous nonconformity, so is Aristophanes seriously threatened in the polis for his plays. Those who see through the disguise, who can understand the playful seriousness of comedy, are the clever ones; those who do not (the Chorus and the Cleons in the audience) are the fools.

In these ways Aristophanes, as dramatist and as citizen, challenges the audience to examine and engage with the theatrical event in which they are participants, so that by becoming more reflective and critical as a theatrical audience they might also become more reflective and critical about their role in assemblies, where they must judge the arguments of a Cleon.

Dicaeopolis's defense-speech convinces half of the Chorus but not the other half, who are worsted in a scuffle and invoke the aid of the military commander, Lamachus. In real life a competent soldier (after his death Aristophanes would praise him without irony as a hero), Lamachus represents the high command generally and is caricatured as the Braggart Soldier. From the safety of his separate peace, Dicaeopolis voices the contempt and the complaints dear to the hearts of common soldiers in any era: we do all the fighting for meager pay and bad rations, while the officers live it up on embassies and high pay. More seriously, Dicaeopolis suggests that such profits, not a just cause, are the real reason for Lamachus' support of the war. In this regard, Lamachus was a good choice for Aristophanes' Braggart Soldier: his name aside (it means "Very Warlike"), Lamachus was the poorest of contemporary commanders and so most vulnerable to Dicaeopolis's accusations of featherbedding.

Dicaeopolis goes off to establish his market, where all traders are welcome—except Lamachus. The rest of the Chorus, now convinced that Dicaeopolis is no traitor, rejoin their fellow Choristers to perform the Parabasis. As is typical in Old Comedy, the episodes following the Parabasis illustrate the success of the hero's plan, leaving behind the conflicts and arguments by which it was achieved. Pointed debate gives way to slapstick. The Chorus henceforth plays the role of commentator, mediating between stage and audience and performing, between episodes, songs that mock individuals among the spectators and that are relatively detached from the plot.

Free to deal with Athens' enemies, Dicaeopolis demonstrates his shrewdness as a trader and his good fortune in being able freely to enjoy what was forbidden to other Athenians because of the war. A starving Megarian is willing to part with his two young daughters for a bunch of garlic and a quart of salt. From a Theban he gets a Copaic eel (a delicacy) in return for an informer, a type much feared by wartime Athenians but whom Dicaeopolis packs up like a piece of pottery. When the Pitcher Feast with its drinking-contest is announced, Dicaeopolis prepares a festive dinner that includes the sort of delicacies that would make most spectators' mouths water. To a farmer who has lost his oxen and a bridegroom who offers to trade a piece of meat Dicaeopolis refuses to share any of his peace, but he does send some to a bride, since women are not responsible for the war.

This exception helps us to understand and to sympathize with Dicaeopolis's refusal to share his peace, which some commentators regard as indefensible selfishness. As we saw in the prologue, Dicaeopolis decided to get his private treaty only after none of his fellow-citizens would heed his call for discussions about peace or come to his aid when he was roughed up by barbarians. They favored the war then; why should they now enjoy the hard-won blessings of Dicaeopolis's peace? Aristophanes seems to be saying to the spectators, "If you want to enjoy what Dicaeopolis has (and who would not?), then you had better stop ignoring or silencing people like him (and like me) and make peace for yourselves." As was argued above, Aristophanes does not want to hold Dicaeopolis's own method up as a model in real life.

The play ends with a memorable confrontation between Dicaeopolis, the man at peace, and Lamachus, the man at war. As Lamachus prepares arms and field-rations to defend the border passes from Boeotian bandits in the dead of winter, Dicaeopolis prepares a sumptuous banquet for the pitcher feast, to which he has been invited by the Priest of Dionysus. Lamachus subsequently returns on a stretcher, wounded by a vine-prop as he leapt over a ditch—a symbolically apt wound for one who opposes Dionysus by rejecting peace and bringing war to the countryside. Lamachus' cries of woe are counterpointed by Dicaeopolis's cries of joy: he enters drunk, supported by a pair of amorous girls, to celebrate his victory in the drinking-contest.

Aristophanes invites the spectators to identify in fantasy with Dicaeopolis and thus indulge in some vicarious wish-fulfillment. For a while an escapist vision lets them forget the hardships of the war. But Aristophanes surely hoped that the urgings of the first part of the play—that the spectators re-examine the rationale for continued war and be more critical of their leaders—would not be forgotten when the spectators left the theater.

Production

Since fifth-century comic poets put on a play for a particular competition and did not envisage future productions, an original script that later circulated as a text for readers contained only the words, with few if any attributions of lines to speakers and no stage directions. These had to be inferred from the words of the text itself, so that all editions and translations, ancient and modern, differ to some extent in reconstructing the theatricality of the text. This means that anyone reading or performing an ancient comedy has a perfect right to bring the text to life in any way that seems appropriate: we have no information external to the text itself about how lines were originally distributed or performed, or about the original action on-stage and in the orchestra. Thus there can be no 'authentic' productions of ancient comedies, only productions that strive, to a greater or lesser degree, to approximate what little we know of performance conditions at the time of their original production. In any case it is pointless to argue about 'authenticity': in the end only satisfied spectators really count.

In this translation I assign speakers who seem to be the likeliest candidates for given lines; the reader is free to differ. I do not, however, supply stage-directions in the text itself: one of the pleasures of reading or performing an ancient comedy is imagining how it might be realized in action. I hesitate to put my own imagination in the way of a reader's, an actor's or a director's. But I do occasionally draw attention, in the notes, to likely action that is not quite obvious from the words of the text.

We do know some facts about fifth-century comic theater, however, and there is no harm in reviewing them for their historical interest.

Although Aristophanes' comedies are highly sophisticated as poetry and as drama, they nevertheless respected some ancient Dionysiac traditions that we should bear in mind if we want to respond to the characters in historical perspective. The actors wore masks, made of cork or papier-mâche, that covered the entire head. These were generic (young man, old woman, etc.) but might occasionally be special, like a portrait-mask of a prominent citizen (as in the case of Socrates in *Clouds*) or an animal or god. Although the characters' clothing was generically suited to their dramatic identities, mostly contemporary Greeks, there were several features that made them unmistakably comic: wherever possible, the costumes accommodated the traditional comic features of big stomach and rump and (for male characters) the grotesque costume penis called the phallos, made of leather, either dangling or erect as appropriate, and circumcised in the case of outlandish barbarians. Apparently by comic convention, male characters appearing without a phallos were marked as being in some way unmanly. And, as in every other dramatic genre, all roles were played by men. Even the naked females who often appear on stage, typically in the traditionally festive ending, were men wearing body-stockings to which false breasts and genitalia were attached. But the convention of all-male actors does not mean that Old Comedy was a kind of drag show: the same convention applied to all other kinds of drama as well (as it still did in Shakespeare's time), and nowhere in our comic texts is any female character ever understood to be anything but the character she is supposed to be, never a male playing a female.

The city supplied an equal number of actors to each competing poet, probably three, and these actors played all the speaking roles. In *Birds*, for example, there are 22 speaking roles, but the text's entrances and exits are so arranged that three actors can play them all. Some plays do, however, require a fourth (or even a fifth) actor in small roles. Perhaps in given years the allotment changed, or novices were periodically allowed to take small parts, or the poet or producer could add extra actors at his own expense.

In the orchestra ('dancing space') was a chorus of 24 men who sang and danced to the accompaniment of an aulos, a wind instrument that had two recorder-like pipes played simultaneously by a specially costumed player; and there could be other instruments as well. Like actors, members of the chorus wore masks and costumes appropriate to their dramatic identity. There could be dialogue between the chorus-leader and the actors on-stage, but the chorus as a whole only sings and dances. There was no ancient counterpart to the 'choral speaking' often heard in modern performances of Greek drama. The choral songs of comedy were in music and language usually in a popular style, though serious styles were often parodied, and the dancing was expressive, adding a visual dimension to the words and music.

The stage-area was a slightly raised platform behind the large orchestra. Behind it was a wooden two-story building called the *skene* ('tent', from which our word 'scene'). It had two or three doors at stage-level, windows at the second story, and a roof on which actors could appear. On the roof was a crane called the *mechane* ('machine'), on which actors could fly

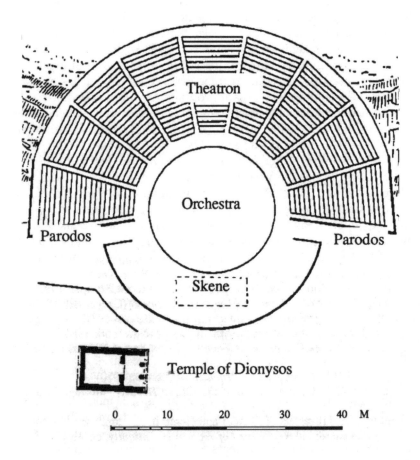

A reconstruction of the Theater of Dionysos in Athens

above the stage (as gods, for example, whence the Latin expression *deus ex machina*, 'god from the machine'). Another piece of permanent equipment was a wheeled platform called the *ekkyklema* ('device for rolling out'), on which actors and scenery could be wheeled on-stage from the skene to reveal 'interior' action. A painted or otherwise decorated plywood facade could be attached to the skene if a play (or scene) required it, and movable props and other scenery were used as needed. Since plays were performed in daylight in a large outdoor amphitheater, all entrances and exits of performers and objects took place in full view of the spectators. All in all, more demand was made on the spectators' imagination than in modern illusionistic theater, so that performers must often tell the spectators what they are supposed to see.

A fifth-century comedy was played through without intermission, the performance probably lasting about two hours. The usual structure of a comedy was a Prologue (actors); the Parodos, or entry, of the chorus into the orchestra (chorus); an Agon, or contest (actors and chorus); the Parabasis, or self-revelation, of the chorus (chorus-leader and chorus); and a series of episodes (actors) articulated by choral songs (chorus). In some plays, like *Clouds*, there can be a second parabasis and/or a second agon. In this translation I have supplied appropriate divisions of the action, but performers should, as always, feel free to arrange their own performance as they see fit.

General Bibliography

Ancient sources for the production of classical drama are collected and discussed in:

Csapo, E. and Slater, W.J. *The Context of Ancient Drama* (Ann Arbor 1995)

Green, J.R. *Theatre in Ancient Greek Society* (London and New York 1994)

Pickard-Cambridge, A.W. *Dithyramb, Tragedy and Comedy*, rev. by T.B.L. Webster (Oxford 1962)

_____ *The Dramatic Festivals of Athens*, rev. by J. Gould and D.M. Lewis (Oxford 1968, rev. 1988)

Taplin, O. *Comic Angels and Other Approaches to Greek Drama through Vase-Paintings* (Oxford 1993)

Walcot, P. *Greek Drama in its Theatrical and Social Context* (Cardiff 1976)

Webster, T.B.L. *Greek Theatre Production* (London 1970)

Good general treatments of Aristophanic comedy are:

Arnott, P. *Greek Scenic Conventions in the Fifth Century B.C.* (Oxford 1962)

Bowie, A.M. *Aristophanes. Myth, Ritual and Comedy* (Cambridge 1993)

Cartledge, P. *Aristophanes and his Theatre of the Absurd* (London 1990)

Dover, K.J. *Aristophanic Comedy* (California 1972)

Harriott, R.M. *Aristophanes, Poet and Dramatist* (Baltimore 1986)

Hubbard, T.K. *The Mask of Comedy. Aristophanes and the Intertextual Parabasis* (Ithaca 1991)

MacDowell, D.M. *Aristophanes and Athens* (Oxford 1995)

McLeish, K. *The Theatre of Aristophanes* (New York 1980)

Moulton, C. *Aristophanic Poetry* (Hypomnemata 68: Göttingen 1981)

Reckford, K.J. *Aristophanes' Old-and-New Poetry* (Chapel Hill 1987)

Russo, C.F. *Aristophanes, an Author for the Stage* (London 1994)

Sifakis, G. *Parabasis and Animal Choruses* (London 1971)

Sommerstein, A.H. et al., eds. *Tragedy, Comedy and the Polis* (Bari 1993)

Stone, L.M. *Costume in Aristophanic Comedy* (New York 1981)

Whitman, C.H. *Aristophanes and the Comic Hero* (Cambridge MA 1964)

Winkler, J.J. and Zeitlin, F.I., eds. *Nothing to Do With Dionysos? Athenian Drama in its Social Context* (Princeton 1990)

Suggestions for Further Reading

Readers interested in the Greek text are referred to the editions with commentary by W.J.M. Starkie (London 1909, repr. Amsterdam 1968); W. Rennie (London 1909); R.T. Elliott (Oxford 1914); A.H. Sommerstein (Warminster 1980), which has an excellent literal translation.

Good treatments of *Acharnians* are:

De Ste. Croix, G.G.M. *The Origins of the Peloponnesian War* (London/ Ithaca 1972), see index and Appendix XXIX.

Edmunds, L. "Aristophanes's Acharnians," in *Yale Classical Studies* 26 (1980)

Foley, H.P. "Tragedy and Politics in Aristophanes's Acharnians," in the *Journal of Hellenic Studies* 108 (1988)

Harriott, R.M. "Aristophanes and the Plays of Euripides," in the *Bulletin of the Institute for Classical Studies* 9 (1962)

————. "The Function of the Euripides-Scene in Aristophanes's *Acharnians*," in *Greece and Rome* 29 (1982)

MacDowell, D.M. "The Nature of Aristophanes's Acharnians," in *Greece and Rome* 30 (1983)

Newiger, H.-J. "War and Peace in the Comedy of Aristophanes," in *Yale Classical Studies* 26 (1980)

Taplin, O. "Tragedy and Trugedy," in the *Classical Quarterly* 33 (1983)

Acharnians

CHARACTERS

SPEAKING CHARACTERS

Dicaeopolis of Cholleidae, a rustic
Herald
Godson, son of Lycinus, an immortal
Ambassador returned from the King of Persia
Pseudo-Artabas, the Persian King's "Eye"
Theorus, a politician
Daughter of Dicaeopolis
Slave of Euripides
Euripides, the tragic poet
Lamachus, a general
Megarian
Girls (two), daughters of the Megarian
Informer
Theban
Nicarchus, another informer
Slave of Lamachus
Dercetes of Phyle, a farmer
Best Man
Messenger I (from the generals)
Messenger II (from the priest of Dionysus)
Messenger III (from the battlefield)

MUTE CHARACTERS

Officers of the Athenian Assembly   Wife of Dicaeopolis
Citizens attending the Assembly   Children of Dicaeopolis
Policemen policing the Assembly   Soldiers under Lamachus
Eunuchs, two   Ismenias, slave of the Theban
Thracian Mercenaries   Pipers from Thebes
Xanthias, slave of Dicaeopolis   Maid of Honor
Slaves of Dicaeopolis   Dancing-Girls, two
Ambassadors returned from the King of Persia

CHORUS

Old Men of Acharnae, twenty-four

PROLOGUE

*(Dicaeopolis, Herald, Godson, Ambassador, Pseudo-Artabas, Theorus; Officers,
Citizens, Policemen, Ambassadors, Eunuchs, Thracian Mercenaries)*

Dicaeopolis
How often have I chewed my heart with rage!
My pleasures? Very few; in fact just four.
My pains? The grains in a million heaps of sand.
Let's try to recall a case of real euphoria.
I know! It's something my heart rejoiced to see: 5
that million-dollar fine coughed up by Cleon°
That really gave me joy! I love the Knights
for that indictment: a banner day for Greece!
But then I had another pain, quite tragic:
I was waiting for a play by Aeschylus,°   10
then heard, "Theognis, bring your chorus on."°

---

6 What had pleased Aristophanes, a personal enemy of Cleon (see Introduction),
   also pleases his hero. But the precise nature of the incident referred to in these lines
   is obscure. Ancient commentaries explain that some island allies had bribed the
   demagogue Cleon to argue for a reduction of their property taxes or tribute and that
   the Knights, motivated by an old grudge, had made him "cough up" the money. If
   so, the case cannot have gone to trial: conviction for bribery would have resulted in a
   more severe penalty and at least some interruption of Cleon's political career. Cleon
   probably made restitution to avoid trial by the procedure known as *probole*. Some
   scholars think that the incident is not historical at all but took place in a comedy,
   perhaps Aristophanes's *Babylonians* (see lines 377 ff.), but that is very unlikely, since
   the Knights do not seem to have played a role in any comedy before *Knights*: see 299
   ff., *Knights* 507 ff..
10 The great tragic poet, who had died thirty years before, was a favorite of older men
   like Dicaeopolis, nostalgic for the empire-building years after the Persian wars. The
   patriotic and inspirational qualities of Aeschylus' plays are dramatized in Aristophanes's *Frogs*.
11 The comic poets nicknamed this "frigid" tragic poet "Snow".

Imagine how that shook up my poor heart!
Another joy was after Moschus played:
Dexitheus did some Theban country-tunes.°
But recently I died and went to hell,   15
when Chaeris played the Anthem on his pipes.°
But never since I first began to wash
with soap have I cried such tears as I cry now,
whenever the Assembly holds a meeting
and all the seats are empty, just like now,   20
while everybody's gossiping in the market
and trying to avoid the summoner.
The Magistrates aren't even here; they're late,
and when they come you can't imagine how
they'll fight each other for the front-row seats,   25
like a river in spate. But as for talk of peace,
not a single moment's thought. My poor, poor Polis!
And I'm the one who always gets here first.
I come and sit, and in my solitude
I sigh, I yawn, I stretch myself, I fart,   30
I fiddle, draw, pick boogers, figure sums;
I watch the countryside and yearn for peace,
I hate the city and want to see my farm,
my village where you never hear "Buy coal,
buy vinegar, buy oil, buy this, buy that."   35
I grow my own and need no Mister Buy.
So now I'm here, all ready to make some noise,
to shout and interrupt and give 'em hell
if anyone speaks of anything but peace!
Hey look, the Magistrates! They're hours late.°   40
What did I tell you? And just as I predicted,
each one is pushing for a front-row seat.

Herald
Move on, move on!
Inside the sacred precinct, all of you!

---

14 Two noted *kithara* (lyre) players; Dicaeopolis's preference was determined by Dex-
    itheus' choice of song.
16 The comic poets considered Chaeris a bad piper and lyre-player.
40 The Herald, Officers, Policemen and Citizens enter, followed by Godson, in the
    Greek "Amphitheus," which means "divine on both sides of the family," so that this
    character's name may simply be a comic invention suitable to his fantastic plot-func-
    tion. But there was a man by that name (its only attestation in Attica), a demesman
    of Aristophanes who is known to have belonged to a club whose members included
    one of Aristophanes's producers and the knight Simon, who is represented by one of
    the choristers in the following year's play, *Knights*.

Godson
Has anybody spoken?

Herald
                    Who wants to speak?   45

Godson
Me.

Herald
  Who are you?

Godson
                    I'm Godson.

Herald
                    Mortal?

Godson
                    No,
immortal. Godson was Demeter's child°
with Triptolemus, the father of Celeus,
the husband of Phaenarete my grandma,
of whom was born Lycinus. Being his son,   50
I'm immortal. And to me the gods entrust
the making of a treaty with the Spartans.
But though immortal, I've got no travel-money;
the Magistrates won't provide it.

Herald
                    Officers!

Godson
Triptolemus and Celeus, see my plight!   55

Dicaeopolis
Oh Magistrates, gentlemen, this is out of line,
arresting the man who wanted to help us get
a treaty of peace, a chance for an armistice!

Herald
Sit down, shut up!

Dicaeopolis
                    I certainly will *not*,
unless you start a discussion about peace.   60

---

47 A genealogy derived from the Mysteries at Eleusis, the most august Attic cult, but so
    comically mangled as to suggest lunatic pretension.

Herald
Ambassadors from the King!°

Dicaeopolis
You and the King! I'm sick of ambassadors
and all their fancy peacocks and their bragging.

Herald
Be quiet!

Dicaeopolis
Eldorado, what a get-up!°

Ambassador
You sent us to the King of Persia's palace,   65
with a salary of a thousand bucks a day,
eleven years ago today—

Dicaeopolis
The waste!

Ambassador
We're tired out from riding on the plains,
meandering about beneath umbrellas,
reclining softly in our carriages.   70
What hell!

Dicaeopolis
I must have been in heaven, then,   *Common Soldier*
reclining in the garbage by the ramparts.°

Ambassador
And when we dined they forced us to drink wine
from crystal flutes inlaid with solid gold,
a vintage pure and fine.

Dicaeopolis
Ancestral polis!   75
You see how these ambassadors laugh at you?

Ambassador
Barbarians, you see, define a man
by how much food and wine he can consume.

---

61 The fabulously wealthy King of Persia. Both Athens and Sparta sought money for
    the war from the King, but old soldiers like Dicaeopolis hated and despised him as a
    barbarian and as their one-time enemy.

64 A group of sumptuously dressed Ambassadors enters; "Eldorado" translates "Ec-
    batana," the wealthy middle-eastern capital of Media.

72 Dicaeopolis represents either one of the common soldiers who stood watch at the
    walls (Thuc. 2.13) or one of the many refugees from the countryside who "took up
    quarters in the towers along the walls or indeed wherever they could find space to
    live in" (2.17), or both.

Dicaeopolis
For us it's sucking cocks and bending over.°

Ambassador
So three years later we got to the Great King's palace,   80
but he'd gone off with his army to take a dump.
He shat for eight whole months in the Golden Hills.

Dicaeopolis
How long did he take to close his royal asshole?
From moon to moon?

Ambassador
                    And then the King came home,
and feasted us with whole oxen, baked   85
in giant ovens.

Dicaeopolis
              And who has ever seen
an oven-baked ox? What absolute baloney!

Ambassador
And then, I swear, he gave us birds three times
the size of Cleonymus; he called them cons.°

Dicaeopolis
That figures, since you're conning all of us.   90

Ambassador
And now we're back, with Pseudo-Artabas,°
the Great King's Eye.

Dicaeopolis
May a crow peck it out with his beak,
and your eye too, you great Ambassador!

Herald
The Great King's Eye!°

Dicaeopolis
                    O holy Heracles!

---

79 Comic poets routinely assumed that successful politicians had prostituted themselves to higher-ranked men for advancement.
89 A political crony of Cleon's, ridiculed by comic poets as a glutton and a coward.
91 The comic "Pseudo-" suggests fraud; Aristophanes's caricature of such Persian officials was calculated to arouse both derisive laughter and indignation at the policy of seeking Persian help in the war.
94 Enter Pseudo-Artabas, accompanied by two eunuchs. He represents the Persian official who held the title, "King's Eye," here taken literally by having a great eye painted on his mask; Dicaeopolis is reminded of a warship's oarports (called "eyes").

Ye gods, what's this? You look just like a warship. 95
You're rounding the point and looking for a berth?
Is that a porthole-flap there under your eye?

Ambassador
So tell us what the King sent you to tell
the Athenians, Oh my Pseudo-Artabas.

Pseudo-Artabas
Iartaman exarxas apisona satra.° 100

Ambassador
You all hear what he says?

Dicaeopolis
                                    I surely didn't.

Ambassador
He says the King is going to send you gold!
Speak louder and more plainly about the gold.

Pseudo-Artabas
No gettum goldum, gapey arse Atheni-o.°

Dicaeopolis
Good Grief, that's pretty plain!

Ambassador
                                    Why? What's he saying? 105

Dicaeopolis
Say what? He says we've all got gaping assholes
if we really expect to get the barbarian gold.

Ambassador
No no! He says, you'll get the gold, no hassle.

Dicaeopolis
What do you mean, no hassle? You're a liar!
Get lost! I'll do the questioning myself. 110
So come clean, Persian, in front of this witness here,
or else I'll dye you Middle Eastern purple:
does the King intend to send us any gold?
So we're being deceived by our ambassadors?
It's very Greek, the way these Persians nod. 115
I wonder if they're not a couple of homeboys.
One of these eunuchs, this one, looks familiar.

---

100 Mock-Persian of doubtful meaning.
104 A "gaping asshole" indicated both unmanly submission and prostitution.

I know him! Cleisthànes son of Sibyrtius!°
Oh you who shave thy hot and horny asshole,
do you, oh monkey, with a beard like yours,   120
show up at assembly decked out like a eunuch?
And who might this other be? It can't be Strato!

Herald
Be quiet! And sit down!
The council's pleased to ask the Great King's Eye
to dine at City Hall.°

Dicaeopolis
             I'm ready to puke!   125
I guess I'm just supposed to hang around
while these guys get the royal welcome mat.
No, I'm going to do a great and awesome deed!
Where'd that Godson get to ?

Godson
                       Over here.

Dicaeopolis
Look, here's a hundred bucks for you to arrange   130
a peace with the Spartans for me and me alone,
for my kiddies too, of course, and the little woman.
You jerks can keep on gaping at Ambassadors.

Herald
Theorus, lately come from Poohbah!°

Theorus
                    Present!

Dicaeopolis
And yet another phony is announced.   135

---

118 Comic poets mocked Cleisthenes as a beardless effeminate, and Strato is elsewhere
    mentioned as his lover. Sibyrtius, who ran a wrestling-school, may really have been
    Cleisthenes' father, but more likely Aristophanes mentions him as a joke. If so its
    meaning is unclear: perhaps the manly sport of wrestling was absurd in connection
    with the pansy Cleisthenes, or perhaps Aristophanes suggests that Sibyrtius had
    enjoyed Cleisthenes sexually: wrestling-schools were prime venues for homosexual
    relationships, and wrestling is a common Greek metaphor for sex.
125 The Prytaneum, in the Agora, which was used to entertain, at public expense,
    foreign ambassadors and Athenians returning from embassies. Individuals could be
    rewarded for especially great services to the state with meals there for life. Within a
    year Cleon was to be so rewarded for the great Athenian victory at Pylos, a victory
    Aristophanes disgustedly claimed (in *Knights*) should rightfully have been credited
    to Cleon's colleague, Demosthenes.
134 "from the court of Sitalces," the King of the Odrysae in Thrace, who had aided the
    Athenians in an abortive invasion of Macedonia four years earlier. Theorus is men-
    tioned elsewhere as a crony of Cleon.

Theorus
    We wouldn't have stayed in Thrace so very long—
Dicaeopolis
    If you hadn't drawn some pretty hefty paychecks.
Theorus
    but the whole of Thrace was shoulder-deep in snow,
    and all the rivers froze at the very same time,
    when Theognis' play was leaving you all cold.°   140
    I stayed on duty, drinking with the Poohbah,
    and I must say he's very pro-Athenian.
    He actually has the hots for you. His walls
    are plastered over with Men of Athens pinups.
    His son, the one we'd made a citizen,   145
    kept pining to be a genuine Greek by blood,°
    and begged his dad to send us aid and succor.
    Poohbah agreed, and swore he'd send an army
    so big that all Athenians would have to say,
    "What a giant swarm of locusts heads our way!"   150
Dicaeopolis
    May lightning strike me if I believe a word
    of what you've said here, except the locust part.
Theorus
    May I present his gift: some mercenaries,
    the nastiest tribe in Thrace.
Dicaeopolis
                            That's plain enough.
Theorus
    Come forward, Thracians that the Poohbah sent.   155
Dicaeopolis
    The hell is this?
Theorus
                    The army of Odomanti.
Dicaeopolis
    Odomanti my ass. What's this supposed to be?
    Who chopped the Odomantians' foreskins off?°

---

140 See 11 n.
146 "yearned to eat blood-pudding at the Apaturia," a festival at which children and
     new citizens became members of Athenian kinship-groups.
158 The Greeks considered circumcision barbaric; these Odomanti were evidently
     equipped with the kind of large, red-tipped phalloi that Aristophanes in *Clouds* men-
     tions in a list of trite ways to get a laugh.

Theorus
> A hundred bucks a day for each of them,°
> and they'll rape the whole of Boeotia with their spears.°   160

Dicaeopolis
> A hundred a day for guys without a foreskin?
> The men who row our ships and guard our polis°
> would yell about that! Hey, dammit! Now I'm done for:
> the Odomantians have swiped my lunch!
> Hey, drop that sandwich!

Theorus
>   Wait, you idiot,   165
> don't rush them when they're in a feeding frenzy!°

Dicaeopolis
> Oh Magistrates, do you let me suffer this
> in my own polis, at the hands of barbarians?
> I move that the Assembly be adjourned
> and the subject of Thracian pay be tabled. I say   170
> I felt a drop of rain, a sign from Zeus.°

Herald
> Depart, you Thracians, return in two days' time.
> The Magistrates say this Assembly is adjourned.

Dicaeopolis
> Alas, alas, what a tasty lunch I've lost!
> But look, here's Godson coming back from Sparta.   175
> Hey Godson, slow down.

Godson
>   Not til it's safe to stop.
> The Acharnians are after me, gotta run!°

Dicaeopolis
> Say what?

Godson
>   I was on my way back with some treaties,

---

159 "two drachmas": absurdly high pay for such mercenaries.

160 For Boeotia, a major enemy of Athens, see 624 n.

162 Rowers on an Athenian warship got one drachma per day.

166 "when they're garlic-primed," like fighting-cocks.

171 Although official business could be suspended by storms, earthquakes or other signs of divine displeasure, such a motion would have to be approved by religious authorities. Here Aristophanes motivates the exit of the assemblymen by making them only too willing to use such a flimsy excuse to adjourn.

177 For the Acharnians, represented in this play by the chorus, see Introduction.

but they got wind of them, some tough old men,   180
Acharnians, as tough as hardwood, veterans
of Marathon. They all started yelling, "Traitor,°
do you bring treaties when our vines are slashed?"
They began to fill their pockets up with stones.
I ran away from there; they chased me, shouting.   185

Dicaeopolis
Well, let them shout. You've got the treaties with you?°

Godson
I do indeed. Three samples for you to taste.
This here's a five-year treaty. Have a sip.

Dicaeopolis
Yuk.

Godson
      What's the matter?

Dicaeopolis
                 I can't stomach this.
It smells of pitch and battleship construction.°   190

Godson
OK then, here's a ten-year treaty. Try it.

Dicaeopolis
But this one smells like embassies to the allies,°
a sour smell, like someone being bullied.

Godson
Well, this one's a treaty lasting thirty years°
by land and sea.

---

182 The battle of Marathon was fought in 490, which would make our Acharnians at
      least 82 years old. But we are not to calculate their claim literally: "Marathon-fight-
      ers" was a conventional comic way to refer to the oldest living generation—the
      generation that repulsed the Persians, established the democracy and acquired the
      empire—by way of contrasting it with the present generation, always portrayed in
      comedy as inferior and less successful.

186 The Greek for "treaty" is *spondai*, literally "libations" of wine, part of the ceremony
      by which a treaty was ratified. Here Aristophanes equates the wines themselves
      with the potential treaties, so that their vintage and character refer also to the length
      and provisions of the treaties.

190 Pitch was used to caulk ships and to flavor inferior wines; the pitchy *retsina* is still a
      common table-wine in Greece.

192 An official delegation from Athens would warn allies tempted to revolt from the
      empire of severe punishment, like that meted out to the people of Mytilene in 428
      (Thucydides 3.1-50).

194 Athens and Sparta had agreed to a thirty-year treaty twenty years earlier; the fifty-
      year treaty agreed to in 421 actually lasted barely six years.

Dicaeopolis
> Sweet feast of Dionysus!   195
> This treaty smells of nectar and ambrosia,
> and never hearing "get your three days' rations."
> It says to my palate "go wherever you like"!
> I accept it; I pour it in libation; I drink it off.
> I tell the Acharnians to go to hell.   200
> For me it's no more hardships, no more war:
> it's home to the farm and a feast for Dionysus!°

Godson
> For me it's getting clear of the Acharnians!

PARODOS I°

Chorus Leader
> This way, everybody, chase him,
>   question every passerby,
> find out where the man has run to,
>   take him into custody!   205
> Do our fatherland a favor.
>   Anybody out there know
> where on earth this man is heading,
>   carrying the peace treaty?

Chorus (1¹)
> He's gone, he's away,
>   his trail is cold.
> It's our misfortune
>   to be so old!   210
>
> When young we could tote
>   our coal by the ton
> and still pace the lead°

---

202 The Country Dionysia, celebrated each winter by the demes (local communities) both urban and rural; because of the war, Dicaeopolis (like many spectators) has been unable to celebrate this festival in his own deme for six years.

204 "Parodos" was technically the word for the path taken by an entering chorus into the orchestra ("dancing-space"), but it came to be used also of the section of a play when this takes place. In *Acharnians*, the parodos is split into two parts by Dicaeaopolis' hymn to Dionysus.
    The songs and dances performed by a Greek dramatic chorus were normally strophic: composed in two or more strophes (stanzas) that had the same rhythmical structure. In this translation, each chorus is numbered consecutively, and each strophe comprising a chorus is numbered by superscript: this is the first strophe of the first chorus (the parodos).

214 "we could have kept up with Phayllus in a race," referring to the famous runner and pentathelete who commanded a ship in the battle of Salamis in 480.

in a marathon.

Were we in pursuit
  when we were young men,   215
we'd never have lost
  the treaty-man then.

Chorus Leader
Now it's different: now because my
  shin's arthritic, now because
old man Lacratides' legs are
  heavy with antiquity,°   220
off he runs. But let's pursue him!
  Never let him laugh to think
slipping us Acharnians is
  easy, though we're very old.

Chorus (1²)
Not he, father Zeus
  and gods on high,
who's made his peace
  with our enemy.   225

For him and his like
  our hatred demands
implacable war
  because of our lands.

We'll never give up
  until like a reed
we pierce them deep
  and painfully,   230

right up to the hilt,
  in vengeance so fine
that never again
  will they trample our vines.

Chorus Leader
Now we've got to find this fellow.
  Look for him in Stonington,°
chase him up and down the country,
  don't give up until he's caught.   235

---

220 One of the choristers, possibly the archon who had held office in the previous cen-
      tury and who was remembered for a record snowfall during his year in office.
234 A pun on Pallene, an Attic deme (202 n.), and *ballein*, "to hit" (here with stones).

I for one could never have my
fill of pelting him with stones.

Dicaeopolis
Silence, holy silence please!

Chorus Leader
Silence, silence, don't you hear the
call for holy silence, friends?
Here's the very man we're seeking.
Move aside and let him through.
Look, it seems the man intends to
hold a sacrificial rite.   240

LYRIC SCENE I
(Dicaeopolis, Dicaeopolis' Daughter, Xanthias, Dicaeopolis' Slaves, Wife and Children)

Dicaeopolis
Silence, holy silence please!
Please, basket-bearer, move ahead a bit.°
Come, Xanthias, hold the phallos nice and straight.°
Put down the basket, dear, and I'll begin.

Daughter
Oh mommy, hand me the ladle here,   245
so I can pour some soup on the sacred cake.

Dicaeopolis
You did that very well. Lord Dionysus,
please smile on this parade and sacrifice
that I and my household celebrate for you.
Good fortune attend our Rural Dionysia   250
and my release from battles. May my thirty
years' peace turn out to be a blessing.
Come, daughter, bear your basket prettily
but make a vinegar face. Ah, lucky the man°
who marries you and begets a litter of pups   255
as good as you at farting in the morning!°

---

242 Basket-bearers in festive processions were typically marriageable young girls; here Dicaeopolis's daughter. Being a basket-bearer was a great distinction and conferred honor on the whole family, so that Dicaeopolis already benefits from his sole possession of peace.

243 A large model of the penis (phallos) was a symbol of fertility and therefore appropriately carried in the procession of a country festival honoring Dionysus.

254 The daughter is told to look solemn in the procession, as if the crowd that would normally watch were present; actually, the watching crowd here are the spectators.

256 "farting" is a surprise substitution for "fucking," implying that the husband will not actually be so "lucky": farting in bed exemplified laziness. Dicaeopolis's jests at

Set forth, and in the crowd hold on to your jewels,
so no one tries to finger you for a snatch.°
And Xanthias, you and your partner have to hold
the phallos erect, behind the basket-bearer.   260
I'll follow along and sing the phallic hymn.
Dear wife, you watch us from the roof. Let's go!

Phales, friend of good old Bacchus,°
   party-mate when evening nears,
lover of lads and lover of lasses,   265
   greetings after six long years!

Glad am I to see my village,
   glad at last to have my peace,
free at last from war and pillage,
   from General Lamachus released!°   270

It's far, far nicer, Phales, Phales,
   to catch a slave-girl stealing coal,
that Thracian girl of Strymodorus,°
   to throw her down and give her a roll
and put her berry on my pole!   275

Phales, Phales,
   if you drink with us and happen to get hung over,
in the morning you'll get a cup of peace to drink,
   and over the fireplace I'll hang my shield.

PARODOS II

(Dicaeopolis, Chorus Leader, Chorus)

Chorus
It's him! It's him!°   280
   Pelt him, pelt him, pelt him, pelt him!

---

   his daughter's expense may sound insulting, but jocular cynicism at the expense of
   brides and bridegrooms is normal in festive contexts.

258 Girls in a procession wore jewelry and so might be targets for thieves; Greek *khrysia*
   (jewelry) puns on *kysos* (vulva).

263 Phales is the personification of the processional phallos (243 n.) and this is the sort
   of song, called *phallikon*, that was typically sung in such a procession. Its uninhibited
   ribaldry was a traditional form of Dionysiac merriment.

270 "Lamachus" means "great warrior" and thus is emblematic of all warriors here. But
   Lamachus was also a real general who will later appear in this play (see 566).

273 Many Athenian slaves were Thracian; the name Strymodorus seems to be generic in
   comedy for old men. Although the activity described here may be mere bravado on
   the part of Dicaeopolis, in reality pretty young slave-girls may well have been at risk
   of being molested or raped by their owners and/or their owners' friends during a
   rowdy wine-festival, especially if caught stealing.

280 The Chorus rushes the procession, sending all but Dicaeopolis into the house.

Hit him, hit the dirty bastard!
  Can't you hit him with your stones?

Dicaeopolis (2¹)°
  Holy Heracles, what's up?
    Watch it, want to smash my cup?

Chorus Leader
  No, you dirty scoundrel you!
    You're the one we want to stone!   285

Dicaeopolis
  Honored old Acharnians,
    what's the cause of all this rage?

Chorus
  What's the reason?
    Shameless man!
  Wretch who betrayed the
    fatherland!
  You alone have   290
    made a peace;
  now you flaunt it
    in my face!

Dicaeopolis
  Want to hear my reasoning?
    want to know why I made peace?

Chorus Leader
  Listen hell! You're dead, my man
    buried under heaps of stones!   295

Dicaeopolis
  Not until you hear my reasons!
    Wait a bit, dear gentlemen!

Chorus
  Nothing doing!
    Save your breath!
  Even Cleon
    we hate less,   300
  Cleon whom we
    plan to slice
  into shoeleather
    for the Knights!°

---

284 This whole lyric interchange between Dicaeopolis and the Chorus
     Leader (284-302) responds rhythmically and structurally with its
     counterpart below (335-46).
302 Here the Chorus suddenly steps out of character (the Acharnians have no reason

Chorus Leader
　I refuse to listen to you!
　　I won't hear you speechify!
　You're the one who treats with Spartans.
　　Now we're going to punish you!

Dicaeopolis
　Gentlemen, forget the Spartans.
　　Put that issue to the side.　　　　　　　　　　305
　Think about the treaty question,
　　whether what I did was right.

Chorus Leader
　How can what you did be righteous,
　　dealing first of all with *them*,
　Spartans who have no respect for
　　gods or oaths or covenants?

Dicaeopolis
　I'm convinced that even Spartans,
　　whom we treat with too much spite,
　can't be held responsible for
　　all the troubles that we have.　　　　　　　　310

Chorus Leader
　Not responsible? You scoundrel!
　　Dare you say that openly,
　right to our face, and after that you
　　think that we would let you off?

Dicaeopolis
　Not for all our troubles, not for
　　all, I said, and in a speech
　I could show you how in some ways
　　we're the party in the wrong.

Chorus Leader
　Dreadful are the words you utter!
　　How they shake me to the heart!　　　　　　　315
　Do you really dare defend our
　　enemies in a speech to us?

---

to hate Cleon) to speak as Aristophanes's own chorus, voicing his hatred of Cleon
and advertising next year's play, *Knights*: for Aristophanes's hatred of Cleon, see
Introduction. "Shoeleather" is a jibe at Cleon's connection with the tanning business,
considered a low, even an immoral trade. Similarly, Dicaeopolis later steps out of
character to speak as actor (416) or on behalf of Aristophanes (377 ff., 499).

Dicaeopolis
> What is more, if I speak wrongly,
>   and the people think I'm wrong,
> I'm prepared to put my head
>   upon a butcher's block and speak.°

Chorus Leader
> Fellow villagers, please tell me
>   why we're hoarding up these stones,
> why we don't unravel him
>   until he's red as a Spartan's coat?   320

Dicaeopolis
> Black the embers of your anger,
>   how they're flaring up anew!
> Won't you listen? Won't you really
>   listen, dear Acharnians?

Chorus Leader
> No we won't, we'll never listen.

Dicaeopolis
> Then you do me grievous wrong.

Chorus Leader
> I would die before I'd listen.

Dicaeopolis
> Don't say that, Acharnians!

Chorus Leader
> Rest assured that you're a dead man.

Dicaeopolis
> Then I'll have to bite you back,   325
>   killing in return the loved one
> who's the dearest of all to you.
> Some of yours I'm holding hostage;
>   I intend to cut their throats!°

---

318 For the parody of Euripides' *Telephus* see Introduction. Here Dicaeopolis literalizes a
metaphor from the play: in fragment 706 Telephus tells Agememnon that he will not
withhold a just reply "even if a man with an axe were about to strike my neck."
   Aristophanes's play *Thesmophoriazusae*, produced in 411, similarly parodies the
plot of Telephus. The fact that Aristophanes could parody a play performed thirteen
years earlier (twenty-seven in the case of *Thesmophoriazusae*) shows that it had been
very memorable. But Aristophanes parodies the tragedy in such a way that even
spectators who had not seen or read it could appreciate the humor; of course, those
who did know the original would better understand the subtleties of Aristophanes's
adaptation.

327 Dicaeopolis goes into the house to get his "hostage"; for the parody see Introduction.

Chorus Leader

> Tell me, fellow villagers, the
> meaning of that speech of his,
> threatening us Acharnians? He
> hasn't got somebody's child,
> one of ours, inside there, has he?
> If he hasn't, why so bold?

Dicaeopolis

> Stone me, if you've got a mind to!
> If you do, I'll slaughter this!
> Soon we'll know if any of you
> feels compassion for his coals!

Chorus Leader

> Now we're really done for! That's a
> charcoal-bucket from my village!°
> Please don't do what you're intending,
> please, oh please, oh please, oh please!

Dicaeopolis (2^2)

> I will kill it. Scream away.
> I won't hear a word you say.   335

Chorus Leader

> You'd destroy my friend, a mere
> innocent philanthracist?

Dicaeopolis

> You refused to hear what I
> had to say a while ago.

Chorus

> Very well, then,
> say your say.
> Tell us clearly
> right away
> why you hold the
> Spartans dear.
> Little bucket,
> we're right here!   340

Dicaeopolis

> First of all, then, please disgorge
> all your stones upon the ground.

---

333 Burning wood for charcoal was a significant industry in the Acharnians' deme.

Chorus Leader
> There they are, they're on the ground.
> Now put down that sword of yours.

Dicaeopolis
> Maybe there's a stone or two
> lurking somewhere in your cloaks.

Chorus
> Look, we've shaken
> out our hoard.
> No excuses:
> now your sword.   345
> Everything is
> on the ground,
> shaken out as I
> dance around.

LYRIC SCENE II

(Dicaeopolis, Chorus Leader, Chorus, Euripides' Slave, Euripides)

Dicaeopolis
> I knew that in the end you'd stop your shouting.
> But some coals from Parnes very nearly died,°
> and all because their friends are acting manic.
> And this bucket, out of fear, has squirted me   350
> with a stream of coal-dust, like a cuttlefish!
> A dreadful thing, that passions should become
> so vinegary that men throw stones and shout
> and are unwilling to listen to all sides,
> when I'm prepared to say, upon a block,   355
> in defence of the Spartans what I have to say.

Chorus (3¹)
> Then get a block and bring it out
> and say what this is all about,
> what's so important as to be
> the grounds for your audacity.   360
> We'd dearly love to understand
> the thought that lies behind your plan.

Chorus Leader
> OK, since you're presiding at this trial,
> set up the block and then begin your speech.°   365

---

348 A spur of Parnes, a heavily forested mountain in northern Attica, extended into
     Acharnae and furnished the wood burned to make Acharnian charcoal.
365 Dicaeopolis goes into the house for a butcher's block.

Dicaeopolis
  All right, then, look: the butcher's block is here,
  and here is little me who's going to speak.
  Don't worry, I won't hide behind a shield,
  but make my case in favor of the Spartans.
  And yet I'm very scared: I know the ways   370
  of farmers, how delightedly they listen
  to any phony speaker with eulogies
  of them and of the polis, true or false.
  They're unaware of being bought and sold.
  I know the minds of the elderly jurors, too: 375
  their only goal is biting with their ballots.°
  And I know myself, what Cleon did to me
  because of the comedy I staged last year.°
  He dragged me in before the Councilors
  and slandered me, tongue-lashing me with lies,   380
  a roaring rapids soaking me with abuse;°
  I nearly drowned in a sewer of litigation.
  So first allow me, before I make my speech,
  to dress myself in a guise most piteous.

Chorus (3²)
  Why twist and turn and scheme this way,
    why this contrivance of delay?   385
  Go ask that pansy sitting there°
    if he would lend a shock of hair,
  a fright-wig shaggy, dark, unclean,
    and wear it so you can't be seen.°   390

---

376 In democratic Athens, full popular sovereignty was rooted in the jury-system, where
     individuals brought lawsuits or prosecutions personally (there were no official
     prosecutors or advocates). Cases were heard by large juries that represented the
     whole people and whose verdict was unappealable. Any citizen 30 or older could be
     a juror and would be paid three obols a day. But this was much less than could be
     earned by work, so that jury-service attracted men unable to work and juries came
     to be composed largely of old men and the urban poor. This arrangement produced
     friction between the generations and social classes: many litigants were wealthy and
     powerful men who resented being at the mercy of a "mob", and jurors might indeed
     use their power vindictively against those they resented, especially when encour-
     aged by demagogues like Cleon. Here Dicaeopolis is concerned with the jurors' sup-
     port of the war. In *Wasps*, produced in 422, Aristophanes satirizes these and other
     problems of the Athenian jury-system.
378 For Cleon's attack on Aristophanes before the Council see Introduction.
381 "roared like the Cycloborus," an Attic stream known for its loudness in spate.
386 They refer to the tragic and dithyrambic poet, Hieronymus, whose long hair opened
     him to abuse as a pathic homosexual. Ancient commentaries note his fondness for
     using frightening masks in his plays.
390 The "cap of Hades" (the lord of the underworld whose name means "unseen") made
     its wearer invisible, just as Hieronymus' hair covers his face.

Chorus Leader
And they expose your trickster's machinations;°
for in *this* contest no one cops a plea.

Dicaeopolis
It's now the time to have a steadfast heart,
and I must go to see Euripides.°
Boy, boy!

Slave
        Who's there?

Dicaeopolis
                Euripides at home?   395

Slave
He is and isn't, if you take my point.°

Dicaeopolis
He is and isn't home?

Slave
           That's right, old man.
His mind is out collecting choice conceits,
while he himself is home, upon the couch,
composing tragedy.

Dicaeopolis
           Lucky Euripides,   400
whose very slave thinks up such clever bits!
Go get him.

Slave
        Can't.

Dicaeopolis
        Go get him anyway.°
I won't go away, I'll knock on the door myself.
Euripides, dear Euripides, answer me,
if ever thou didst answer any mortal!   405

---

391 "your Sisyphean strategems": Sisyphus, a mythical king of Corinth, was legendary
for his craftiness and reportedly had even cheated Death itself.

394 The central stage-door now represents Euripides' house, where Dicaeopolis hopes
to get the costume and props necessary for his "performance." In Old Comedy, a
fantastic rather than a naturalistic kind of drama, such miraculous changes of place
and suspensions of action are common.

396 Among tragic poets, Euripides is especially fond of such paradoxical phrases, here
comically aped by his slave.

402 The slave shuts the door in Dicaeopolis's face.

It's Dicaeopolis from Cholleidae here.°

Euripides
I'm busy.

Dicaeopolis
Please, have yourself wheeled out.°

Euripides
No way.

Dicaeopolis
Please do.

Euripides
Oh, very well. Too busy to leave the couch.

Dicaeopolis
Euripides—

Euripides
Why criest thou?

Dicaeopolis
You compose   410
feet up, not down? No wonder you're fond of cripples!°
And why are you dressed in all those tragic rags,
a raiment piteous? No wonder you like beggars!
Euripides, I beg on bended knee,
please give me a bit of rag from that old play.°   415
I've got to make a long speech to the Chorus,
and if I fail, it means my certain death.

---

406 Here the audience first learns the hero's name. The deme Cholleidae was not far
     from Acharnae; why Dicaeopolis is associated with Cholleidae is unclear. It may
     simply pun on cholos ("lame"), though the idea of lameness has yet to be introduced
     (411).
408 The *ekkyklema* was a platform that could be wheeled on stage to reveal indoor action;
     here Euripides' house is envisioned as having the same apparatus as a stage-house.
     The following action shows that Euripides was revealed reclining on a couch; near
     to hand were raggedy costumes and props, perhaps hanging on a plywood panel
     behind the couch.
411 Aristophanes often exploits the popular idea that what is true of an artist's creations
     must also be true of the artist himself. In his plays, Euripides often confounded con-
     ventional notions about the connection between outward status and inward virtue;
     one of his methods was to portray noble personages crippled or in rags; examples
     follow.
415 Dicaeopolis's inability to recall the name of Telephus, the hero he has in mind,
     allows Aristophanes both to create suspense (at least some spectators would not
     yet have recognized the parody) and to have fun with six other pitiable Euripidean
     characters.

Euripides
Which ragged garb? Not that wherein this Oeneus,
the star-crossed ancient, trod upon the boards?°

Dicaeopolis
No, not from Oeneus; someone still more wretched.   420

Euripides
From Phoenix, that was blind?°

Dicaeopolis
                              Not Phoenix, no,
from someone even wretcheder than that.

Euripides
What tattered raggedness doth the fellow seek?
Then meanest thou the cripple Philoctetes?°

Dicaeopolis
No, no, it's someone much, much cripplier.   425

Euripides
Then does thou wish the foul accoutrement
that this Bellerophon, the cripple, wore?°

Dicaeopolis
No, not Bellerophon, though my man too
was lame, a beggar, glib, a forceful speaker.

Euripides
I know, 'twas Mysian Telephus.°

Dicaeopolis
                              It was!   430
Ah, give me, I beg you, Telephus' swaddlings.

Euripides
Boy, give him the tattered rags of Telephus.

---

419 Oeneus, aged king of Calydon, was deposed by his brother Agrius after the death of
       his only surviving son, Tydeus, and became an impoverished exile. Euripides' play
       told how Tydeus' son, Diomedes, expelled Agrius and restored Oeneus.
421 Phoenix, prince of Hellas, was falsely accused by his father's concubine of trying to
       seduce her; his defense-speech was unconvincing, and he was blinded and exiled.
424 Philoctetes, who accompanied the Greeks to Troy, was cast ashore on the island of
       Lemnos because of a wound in his foot that stank and would not heal. Euripides had
       portrayed him as living for ten years on the charity of the Lemnians until he was
       recalled to Troy as the result of a prophecy. In Sophocles' extant play *Philoctetes*, by
       contrast, the island is deserted and the hero lives on what he can shoot with his bow.
427 The hero Bellerophon, who rode the winged horse Pegasus, tried to fly to heaven but
       was unhorsed by a gadfly sent by Zeus and ended his days as a cripple. Bellero-
       phon's ride is parodied in Aristophanes's play *Peace*.
430 See 318 n.

They're closeted above Thyestes' rags,°
twixt them and Ino's.

Slave

Here they are, they're yours.°

Dicaeopolis
O Lord that seest through and under all—   435
[may I dress myself in guise most piteous.]°
Euripides, since you've been so kind to me,
I'd also like what goes along with these,
the little Mysian beanie for my head.°
The crippled beggar must I play today: 440
be what I am, yet seem to be another.
The audience will know me for who I am,
while the Chorus stands there like a bunch of fools:
with my pointed phrases I'll be giving them the finger.°

Euripides
Then take, for thy gross mind doth finely plan.   445

Dicaeopolis
God bless you, and my best to Telephus, too.
That's good: I'm filling up with wit already!
But I can't go on without a cripple's cane.

Euripides
Then take, and hie thee from these marble halls.

Dicaeopolis
My soul, thou seest how I'm driven from the halls   450
while I still need lots of props, so now be whiny
and wheedly and beggarly. Euripides,
I need a basket burnt through by a lamp.

Euripides
What need, poor wretch, to have such wickerwork?

---

433 Euripides' *Thyestes* evidently dramatized the hero's life as an exile after his brother
      Atreus had expelled him from Mycenae.
434 Athamas, a Thessalian king, believing that his wife Ino (daughter of the Theban
      king, Cadmus) had died, remarried. When he found out that Ino was alive, he had
      her seized and imprisoned; Euripides had evidently staged her in ragged prison-
      clothes.
436 = 384, which however makes less sense in this context and must therefore have been
      mistakenly inserted by a scribe.
439 "Mysian": During Dicaeopolis's speech in disguise, this prop will keep the issues of
      identity and foreignness in the spectators' minds.
444 For Dicaeopolis's distinction between the Chorus, who will be fooled, and the spec-
      tators, who will not be, see Introduction.

Dicaeopolis
No need to have it, I want it anyway.   455

Euripides
Know thou art irksome, and depart my halls.

Dicaeopolis
Ah!
Be fortunate, as once your mother was.°

Euripides
And now begone!

Dicaeopolis
                        I need just one thing more,
a tiny goblet with a broken lip.

Euripides
Take it to blazes, thou troubler of my halls!   460

Dicaeopolis
You don't yet know how troublesome you are.
Please, sweetest Euripides, give me one thing more,
this little bottle cappered with a sponge.

Euripides
You'd rob me, creature, of all my tragedy!
Take this and then depart.

Dicaeopolis
                        I'm on my way.   465
But wait! There's one thing more that, if I fail
to get, I'm lost. My sweetest Euripides,
if this I get I'm gone and won't be back:
I want some withered lettuce for my basket.

Euripides
Thou killest me! Here you are! My plays are gone!   470

Dicaeopolis
No more; I'm off. Indeed I've been a bother,
though little knew I the kings mislike me so.
Good heavens me, I'm ruined! I forgot
the crucial thing on which my fate depends.
My sweetest darling, dear Euripides,   475
may lightening strike me if I ask again,
save this one thing and this one thing alone:

---

457 In reality, Euripides' mother was high-born, but Aristophanes often portrays her as an
impoverished street-vendor of wild herbs (and therefore as conventionally dispute-
table). Whether this portrayal has any connection with reality is unknown.

give me some chervil from thy mother's stall.°

Euripides
The man's insulting. Shoot the gated bolts!°

Dicaeopolis
My soul, sans chervil must we hit the road.°   480
Knowest what a contest you must soon contest,
by speaking in defence of Spartan foes?
Forward, my soul, get on the mark. Right here.
You're standing still? Move out: you've had a shot
of Euripides! That's it! Come, foolish heart,   485
go over there and offer them your head
when you've told them how you think the matter stands.
Be bold. Go on. Move out. I applaud my heart!

LYRIC SCENE III
(Chorus, Dicaeopolis, Chorus Leaders, Lamachus, Lamachus' Soldiers)

Chorus (4¹)
What will you do? What will you say?
You are a shameless, you are an iron man,   491

you who offer your own neck to the city
and plan to speak alone against us all.

Steady he stays, facing his task.
As you have chosen, so must you speak out now.   496

Dicaeopolis
Do not be angry, you men who watch the play,
if, though a beggar, I speak before Athenians°
of state affairs while making comedy.°
For comedy too concerns itself with justice,   500
and what I say will shock you but be just.
And this time Cleon won't make allegations

---

478 See 457 n.
479 Euripides is wheeled inside on the ekkyklema (408 n.).
480 Epic and tragic heroes address their hearts or souls but never get a recalcitrant response!
498 The original lines from *Telephus* (fragment 703) are
> Do not be angry, leaders of the Greeks,
> if, though a beggar, I speak before nobility.
499 The opening, and much of the rest, of this speech is modelled on the speech of Telephus to the Greeks, in which he had claimed that the Mysians were justified in defending themselves and so could not be called traitors. Dicaeopolis similarly defends himself against the Acharnians' charge of treason, as, behind him, the poet defends himself against Cleon's charges. See further Introduction.

that I slander the polis in front of foreigners;
for we're alone, it's a Lenaean competition,
the foreigners aren't yet here, nor tribute-money   505
nor allied troops from the cities of our empire,°
but now we're by ourselves, like grain that's hulled:
I count the immigrants as civic bran.°
Myself, I hate the Spartans with all my heart,
and hope the god Poseidon once again   510
will send a quake that shakes their houses down.°
I too have vines the Spartans have cut down.
But friends—for there are only friends here listening—
why blame these things entirely on the Spartans?
It was men of ours—I do not say our polis;   515
remember that, I do not say our polis—
but some badly-minded troublemaking creeps,
some worthless counterfeit foreign currency,°
who started denouncing shirts from Megara°
and if they spotted a cucumber or a bunny   520
or piglets, cloves of garlic, lumps of salt,
it was Megarian, grabbed, sold off that very day.
Now that was merely local; small potatoes.
But then some young crapshooters got to drinking°
and went to Megara and stole the whore Simaetha.°   525

---

506 Since the sea was dangerous in winter, few non-resident foreigners or allied troops
    would attend the Lenaea, as they did the City Dionysia (see Introduction), where
    tribute payments from Athens' subject allies were officially witnessed by the Athe-
    nians and when allied troops would be mustered for the campaign-season.
508 The citizens are compared to unsifted flour, in which some bran (immigrant non-citi-
    zens) would remain after the milling.
511 In 464 Sparta had been devastated by a great earthquake that many attributed to the
    anger of the god Poseidon following the Spartans' execution of some of their subject
    populace (helots), who had taken refuge in his temple at Cape Taenarum.
518 The metaphor from counterfeit coin amounts to an accusation that the men in question
    are not Athenian by birth and are therefore not entitled to citizen rights, such as
    prosecuting black-marketeers (next n.).
519 Goods from Megara were contraband in Athens by the provisions of a decree that
    the Spartans, on the eve of the war, had demanded the Athenians rescind as being
    provocative; the Athenians, on the urging of Pericles, had refused. Informers who
    prosecuted men in possession of contraband are denounced here as acting not from
    the acceptable motives of personal enmity or the public interest but as extortionists
    and blackmailers. Such an informer is portrayed later in the play (818 ff.).
524 In the party-game *kottabos*, drinkers would try to hit targets with wine-lees thrown
    from their cups.
525 Ancient commentators say that this prostitute counted among her lovers Alcibiades
    (716 n.), whose mother's cousin was Pericles, in whose house he was raised. At this
    time he was prominent among the ambitious young prosecutors later criticized

And then the Megarians, garlic-stung with passion,
got even by stealing two whores from Aspasia.°
From this the origin of the war broke forth
on all the Greeks: from three girls good at blow-jobs.
And then in wrath Olympian Pericles°   530
did lighten and thunder and turn Greece upside-down,
establishing laws that read like drinking-songs:
"Megarians shall be banned from land and markets
and banned from sea and also banned from shore."°
Whereupon the Megarians, starving inch by inch,°   535
appealed to Sparta to help make us repeal
the decree we passed in the matter of the whores.
But we refused although they repeatedly asked.
And then it came to a clashing of the shields.
You say they shouldn't have; but what instead?   540
Come, what if a Spartan spotted a puppy imported
from Seriphus, then denounced it and sold it off,°
would you have calmly sat at home? Far from it!
Why, you'd have instantaneously despatched
three hundred ships; the city would be filled   545
with shouting soldiers, clamor for the skippers,
with pay disbursed, with figureheads being gilded,
with noisy markets, rations being rationed,
with wallets, oarloops, people buying jars,
with garlic, olives, onions packed in nets,   550
with crowns, anchovies, dancing-girls, black eyes,
with the dockyard full of oarspars being planed
and dowelpins hammered, oarports being drilled,
with pipes and bosuns, whistles and tootle-oo.

by the Chorus (676 ff.). By tracing the origins of the present war to woman-steal-
ing, Dicaeopolis parodies a mythological motif found in the *Iliad*, in tragedy and
in Herodotus' *Histories*. In his speech (499 n.), Telephus may well have questioned
the justice of the Trojan War, fought to recover Menelaus' wife Helen, who had
absconded to Troy with Paris as his reward for judging in the goddess Aphrodite's
favor in a beauty-contest.

527 Aspasia was a well-educated and free-born immigrant from Miletus who for many
years lived with Pericles as his lover. Comic poets insinuated that she procured
women for Pericles or even (as here) that she was a trainer of courtesans.

530 Because of Pericles' long career as the leading statesman of Athens, comic poets like
to portray him as a Zeus-like ruler (or tyrant); here the war is attributed to personal
(and sordid) motives.

534 For this decree see 519 n. Dicaeopolis's version of the decree is modelled on an actual
drinking song (by Timocreon of Rhodes.).

535 A starving Megarian will later appear (730 ff.).

542 This small Cycladic island was one of the least important Athenian allies.

I know that's what you'd do: and do we think   555
that Telephus would not? Then we lack sense!°

Leader of First Semichorus

Is that right, you damnable scurvy villain you?
Do you, a beggar, dare say this of us,
and, if there be the odd informer, blame us?

Leader of Second Semichorus

He does, by god, and everything he says   560
is just; in no particular does he lie.

Leader of First Semichorus

Well, even so, had he any right to say it?
He won't be glad that he dared to say such things!

Leader of Second Semichorus

Hey you, where are you running? Stop! Don't hit
this man, for if you do you'll soon get yours!   565

First Semichorus (4²)

Yo, Lamachus, o lightning of eye,°
come to our aid, o thou of the fearsome crest!
Yo, Lamachus, thou friend and fellow tribesman,
or any other officer, general or
stormer of walls, come to our aid,   570
anyone, quickly: we're in a strangle hold!

Lamachus

Whence came this martial din upon mine ear?
Where must I help? Where throw the hurly-burly?
Who's roused my Gorgon from her carrying-case?°

Dicaeopolis

Heroic Lamachus! What crests, what ambushes!   575

Leader of First Semichorus

O Lamachus, has this man not for hours
been spewing slander on our entire polis?

---

556 Dicaeopolis lays his head on the block; half the Chorus move toward him, the other
　　half intervene.
566 In addition to having a warlike name (270 n.), Lamachus was a good choice to exem-
　　plify the military establishment because he was the least wealthy of the contempo-
　　rary commanders and thus best suited Aristophanes's argument that the military
　　leadership, like the politicians, favored the war not out of concern for the people's
　　interest and safety but rather to line their own pockets.
574 Lamachus' shield, which he says he has just now uncased, bore the blazon of a Gor-
　　gon, a mythical female monster whose face literally petrified anyone who saw it.

Lamachus
How dare you, you mere beggar, say such things?

Dicaeopolis
Heroic Lamachus, please be merciful
if I, a beggar, spoke and prattled some.

Lamachus
What did you say of me? Well?

Dicaeopolis
                                    Can't recall: 580
your terrifying armor makes me dizzy.
I beg you, take away that bogyman!

Lamachus
There.

Dicaeopolis
          Lay it upside-down in front of me.

Lamachus
                                    OK.

Dicaeopolis
Now from your helmet take a feather.

Lamachus
So here's a feather.

Dicaeopolis
                          Now please hold my head,   585
so I can puke. Your crests are sickening!

Lamachus
Hey, what're you doing? Use my feather to puke?

Dicaeopolis
What feather is this? Tell me from what bird
this feather comes: perhaps the roaring boastard?

Lamachus
Oh! Now you die!

Dicaeopolis
                        Oh no no, Lamachus,   590
I don't doubt that you're strong. Though if you are,
why don't you skin my cock? You're well equipped.°

---

592 An insulting double-meaning. In one sense "skin my cock" refers to circumcision,
    regarded by the Greeks as a barbaric mutilation, which Dicaeopolis invites Lama-
    chus to perform with his sword. In the other it refers to retraction of the foreskin
    by stimulating an erection, and "well equipped" refers to Lamachus' stage-phallos,
    which Dicaeopolis (in double-meaning) professes to find arousing.

Lamachus
Do you, a beggar, say this to a general?

Dicaeopolis
What, me a beggar?

Lamachus
Well, what are you then?

Dicaeopolis
What am I? A solid citizen, no placehunter,   595
and ever since the war began, a soldier;
while you've become Lord Lofty Salary.

Lamachus
They elected me—

Dicaeopolis
A bunch of cuckoos did!
That sickened me and drove me to make peace,
the sight of greybeards fighting in the ranks   600
and strapping men like you avoiding battle:
those drawing mega-pay on the Thracian coast,
those General Puffers and slippery Sgt. Bilkos,
those guys with Chares, those in Suckerville,°
those Captain Bullshots, Colonel Racketeers,   605
those way out west in Scamtown or in Jokeville.

Lamachus
They were elected.

Dicaeopolis
But what's the reason, then,
that you guys always get paid missions somewhere,
but these folks never do? Say, Mr. Coaldust,°
you're pretty old: did you ever get a mission?   610
He hasn't, though he's solid and works hard.
And what of Coalson, Porter, or Oakwood there:
has any of you seen Ecbatana or Chaonia?°

---

604 Chares is otherwise unknown. "Suckerville" translates "Chaonians," a fierce people
   of Epirus with whom Athens was apparently negotiating. Their name is intended to
   remind us of the verb *khaskein*, "to gape" (be gullible).
606 "in Camarina and Gela and Catagela": the first two are actual towns in Sicily, Cam-
   erina being presently among the towns allied with Athens against Syracuse and her
   allies (including Gela). Gela reminds us of *gelos* ("laughter"), and Catagela (literally
   "lower Gela") is an invented name modelled on *katagelos* ("derision").
609 The Acharnians, here addressed by Dicaeopolis, are given invented names appropriate
   to their chief local industry (333 n.).
613 For Ecbatana see 64 n.; for Chaonia 604.

They haven't. Lamachus and the bluebloods go,°
though yesterday their friends were warning them, 615
because they owe back-taxes and old debts,
to get out of the way, like people dumping slops.°

Lamachus
Democracy, can such talk be endured?

Dicaeopolis
Hell no, unless our Lamachus draws his pay!

Lamachus
Well, I for one on all the Peloponnesians 620
will wage the war and harry them everywhere
with ships and troops to the utmost of my power.

Dicaeopolis
And I proclaim to all the Peloponnasians,
to the Megarians and to the Boeotians too,°
that they can trade with me, but not with Lamachus. 625

PARABASIS°
(Chorus Leader, Chorus)

Chorus Leader
The man has triumphed with his logic;
    he's convinced the populace
about the treaty. Let's strip down, then,
    let's essay the anapests.°

In all the time since our producer's
    been staging comic choruses,
he's never faced the audience

---

614 "L. and the son of Coisyra": Megacles, like Pericles a member of the wealthy aristo-
    cratic family of the Alcmaeonidae, is identified this way to emphasize his non-Athe-
    nian ancestry on his mother's side: Coisyra was of Eretrian origin, having probably
    come to Athens as a small child in 490, when Eretria was occupied by the Persian
    invaders.
617 Lamachus' debts will have resulted from his poverty (566 n.), Megacles' from his
    extravagance.
624 Since both Megara and Boeotia were enemies of Athens, none of their goods could be
    imported or traded. But now that Dicaeopolis is at peace he will be free to trade with
    whomever he likes, and we will presently see him trading with a Megarian and a
    Boeotian.
626 Lamachus exits with his men, Dicaeopolis goes into his house. The Chorus then per-
    forms their parabasis (self-relevation), a traditional structural feature of Old Comedy
    that typically occurs when the initial plot-conflict is settled. It was the Chorus' big
    production-number; thereafter they no longer play an important role in the action,
    but merely sing songs to articulate episodes.
627 The Chorus removed items of clothing before dancing or other vigorous movement,
    such as was required in a parabasis.

to claim superior cleverness.°
But now his enemies have denounced him
    before Athenians quick to judge,   630
as one who ridicules our city
    and insults its citizens.°
So now he asks to plead his case to
    Athenians with open minds.
Our poet says that he deserves your
    thanks for many benefits:
he's stopped you being taken in too
    easily by foreigners
and taking joy in flatterey and
    being sucker-citizens.   635
When ambassadors from allied cities
    used to come to hoodwink you,
they'd start by calling you "violet-crowned,"°
    and every time they called you that
at once that little word would get you
    sitting on your buttock-tips.
And if in buttering you up some
    speaker said that Athens "gleams,"
you'd give him anything he asked, for
    honoring you like mere sardines.   640
For doing that our poet merits
    thanks for many benefits,
for showing what democracy meant for
    peoples of the allied states.°

---

629 This play, like Aristophanes's first two plays, was produced by Callistratus, but the Chorus Leader speaks of poet and producer interchangeably. *Knights* 512-13, where Aristophanes says that "many people" had long been asking him why he had not yet produced plays on his own, is evidence that he was known to be the author of the plays produced by Callistratus.

    A parabasis usually (as here) consisted of a prelude (626-7) and a speech by the Chorus Leader typically written in (and thus referred to simply as the) anapests (628-64); and an epirrhematic syzygy: a strophe (204 n.) by the Chorus followed by an epirrhema (speech) by the Chorus Leader, then a responding antistrophe and antepirrhema ("syzygy" designates the ABAB structure). In the "anapests" the Chorus Leader typically speaks on behalf of the poet: praising his skill, denigrating his rivals and often offering the spectators good advice. In the syzygy the Chorus, in character, address their own complaints and advice to the spectators.

632 Referring to Cleon's denunciation (see Introduction).

637-9 These two terms of praise for Athens came from a poem by Pindar and had evidently become patriotic cliches.

642 Since we do not have *Babylonians*, in which Aristophanes had treated this subject, we cannot know whether he refers to poor democratic self-government in the allied states or to poor Athenian administration of them, or both.

And that's why people from the allies
   bearing tribute for you all
will come to Athens: just to see the
   poet who's the best of all,
who took the risk of speaking to the
   Athenians what is right and just.   645
So far, so wide has news of his great
   courage spread already that
the Persian King himself, when testing
   out the Spartan embassy,°
first asked them which combatant was the
   stronger in her naval force,
then asked them which combatant was the
   target of this poet's abuse;
"for these," he said, "are people who've been
   turned into much better men,   650
and they will be decisive victors,
   having him to give advice."
And that's the reason why the Spartans
   want you now to treat for peace
and ask that you return Aegina:°
   not to get the island back,
they're not concerned with that, they only
   want this poet for themselves.°
But don't you ever let him go,
   for in his plays he'll say what's right.   655
He says he'll give you good instruction,
   bringing you true happiness,
and never flatter, never tempt you,
   never diddle you around,
deceive or soften you with praise, but
   always say what's best for you.
That said, let Cleon hatch his plots
   against me, let him do his worst;   660
for what is right and just shall be

647 The Spartans had in recent years sent embassies to Persia for financial help against
    Athens.
653 Early in the war Athens had expelled the people of this island (near Attica) and
    replaced them with Athenian colonists; the Spartans had given the exiles refuge and
    demanded their restoration.
654 Evidently Aristophanes had some connection with Aegina (family or property), but its
    nature is unknown. These lines strongly suggest that in his attack on Aristophanes
    (see Introduction) Cleon had questioned his Athenian citizenship.

my ally, nor will I be found
to be a citizen like him,
a coward and a punk-ass.°

Chorus (5¹)

This way come, blazing Muse,   665
wield the force of fire,
vehement, Acharnian!

Like a spark that leaps aloft
from oaken coals when roused
by the bellows' favoring wind,
and meat for the grill lies by,   670
and cooks stir up fine relish
agleam with pickle-jewels
and knead the dough:

this way come, sing a song
rousing, ardent, rustic,
to us your deme compatriots!   675

Chorus Leader

We ancient geezers have a gripe to
    lodge against the city.
Unworthily of all the naval
    battles we have fought in,
we get no care as aged men but
    suffer dire treatment.
Although we're elderly you throw us
    into courtroom trials,
allowing us to be the sport of
    stripling prosecutors,   680
old men who're nothing now, as mute as
    broken worn-out trumpets,
whose rod and staff that comfort us is
    just the cane we lean on,
so old that when we stand in court we
    mutter only mumbles
and see before us nothing but the
    foggy gloom of justice.
The stripling, who has cut a deal to

---

664 Greek *katapygon*, designating a man who allows another man to penetrate him anally, need not be taken in its strict sense (though comic poets routinely assume that popular politicians had sold their bodies to get ahead, cf. 79 and 716 nn.), since it was conventionally applied to weak, shameless or meretricious behavior generally.

make the case against him,   685
attacks him quickly, pelting him with
   hard and rounded phrases;
and then he drags him up for questions,
   setting verbal pitfalls,
assaulting, pounding, shaking up a
   ghostly old Tithonus.°
The victim mumbles his reply and
   totters off convicted.
And then he groans and then he weeps, and
   says to his companions,   690
"The fine I owe must come from money
   saved to buy my coffin."

Chorus (5²)
How is this fair or right,
ruining a greybeard
in court beside the water-clock?°

He has borne his share of toil,
he has wiped off manly sweat   695
by the bucket when he fought
for the city at Marathon.°
In our prime, at Marathon,
we pursued the enemy.
But nowadays

evil men eagerly   700
sue and pursue us.
What can the shysters say to this?°

Chorus Leader
Yes, where's the fairness when a stooping
   old Thucydides is
destroyed by being grappled by this
   wilderness of Asia,
I mean Cephisodemus' son, that

---

688 Tithonus, mortal husband of the goddess Dawn, asked Zeus for immortality but forgot
   to include agelessness, so that eventually he withered away to a mere squeaking
   voice.
693 In the lawcourts, the length of each litigant's speech was timed by allowing the same
   amount of water to run out of a container specially designed for that purpose.
697 See 182 n.
702 They mention Marpsias, ridiculed elsewhere in comedy as a troublesome orator and
   parasite. The name, otherwise unattested, means "Grappler" and so is probably a
   nickname.

smooth-tongued prosecutor?°   705
I felt great pity, wiped away a
    tear as I beheld the
old gentleman so hard beset by
    nothing but an archer.
But when that old Thucydides was
    younger, by Demeter,
he'd not have been as easy mark for
    any adversary.
No, first he'd wrestle to the canvas
    ten such prosecutors,°   710
and then he'd lift his voice and bellow
    down three thousand archers,
and then outshoot the kinsmen of the
    prosecutor's father.
But since you won't allow the old a
    peaceful night of sleeping,
at least you ought to change the law to
    make indictments separate:
for old defendants, prosecutors
    just as old and toothless,   715
for youths an Alcibiades, the
    glib-tongued little pansy.°
In future, if there's banishment or
    someone owes the city,
let oldsters charge the oldsters, let the
    youngsters charge the youngsters.

---

705 Thucydides, son of Milesias, now nearly eighty years old, had twenty years earlier
    been the most important of Pericles' political rivals but was exiled in 443 for ten
    years. When he returned he tried to make a comeback by prosecuting Pericles'
    friend, Anaxagoras the philosopher. But his career came to an end in the trial men-
    tioned here, when for some reason he became tongue-tied and was unable to make
    his defence speech. The son of Cephisodemus was Euathlus, mentioned elsewhere in
    comedy for his zeal for prosecution; another of his victims was the sophist Protago-
    ras. The references here to Asian archers play upon gossip or accusations that Cephi-
    sodemus (and therefore his son) had Scythian blood. Scythians were barbarians and
    noted for their skill at archery; many Scythian slaves were used by the city of Athens
    as policemen.
710 A metaphor appropriate to this family: Melesias (705 n.) had been a distinguished
    trainer of wrestlers, and Thucydides' own sons were the leading Athenian wrestlers
    of their time.
716 See 525 n. "Pansy" translates *euryproktos* ("having a wide ass-hole"), an insult often
    enough applied to popular politicians (79 and 664 nn.) but here especially appropri-
    ate for Alcibiades, who was notorious for both homosexual and heterosexual excess.

EPISODE I
(Dicaeopolis, Megarian, Girls, Informer)

Dicaeopolis
These stones will mark the boundary of my market.
It's open for trade to all the Peloponnesians,   720
to all Megarians and Boeotians too,°
provided they trade with me, not Lamachus.
As trade commissioners I appoint these three
duly elected straps from Whippington.°
And let no squealers try to enter here,   725
nor any other species of canary°
I'll fetch the pillar with my treaty inscribed
and display it clearly in my market-place.°

Megarian°
Hello, Athenian market, dear to Megara!
I need you—holy friendship!—like a mommy.   730
You dirty little brats, go get some chow
for your poor dad, if you can turn some up.
And listen! Give me your undivided bellies:
you wanna be sold or friggin starve to death?

Girls
Sold, sold!   735

Megarian
I'd say the same. But who'd be dumb enough
to pay a cent for merchandise like you?
So I've cooked up a real Megarian scam:°

---

721 see 624 n.
724 "from Leproi," a fictitious place-name chosen for its connection with *lepein*, "peel,"
    Athenian slang for "flog." Since Dicaeopolis's market is private he will have to
    enforce its laws himself rather than, as he would in reality, by appealing to the mar-
    ket-commissioners.
726 For informers see 519 n. "Canary" (modern slang for informer) translates *phasianos*,
    "pheasant" or "man from Phasia" with a play on phasis, "denunciation."
728 Dicaeopolis goes inside; a shabbily dressed Megarian enters with his two young
    daughters.
729 For the decree that has impoverished Megara see 519 n. This Megarian speaks in his
    local dialect, a member of the Doric family of dialects that included Spartan Laco-
    nian. Since the Athenians considered Megarians stupid and crude ("Megarian jokes"
    occupying the same category as modern "Polish jokes"), I have given this Megarian
    a coarse sound.
738 The Megarians had a reputation for low trickery.

I'll pass you off as pussycats for sale.°
Put on these collars with the little bells,   740
and look like kitties from a purebred cat.
'Cause, by the God of Traders, you get home
unsold, I'll starve you both to death myself!
Now put these whisker-patches on your mugs,
and then climb up here into this here sack,   745
and do a little yowling and meowing.
Make just like kitties at the kitty-show.°
I'll yell around for Dicaeopolis.
Hey Dicaeopolis, wanna buy some kittens?

Dicaeopolis
What's this? A Megarian?

Megarian
                          Yeah, I've come to trade.   750

Dicaeopolis
How goes it there?

Megarian
                          We sit in the bar and shrink.°

Dicaeopolis
That's nice, by god, if there's a live band there.
What else is new in Megara?

Megarian
                          Same old stuff.
When I hit the road to make the trip up here,
the government was doin' all they could   755
to see that we get totally destroyed.

Dicaeopolis
You'll soon be out of trouble, then!

Megarian
                          That's right.

---

739 Throughout this scene Aristophanes plays on the double sense of Greek *khoiros* "pig"
    (a staple meat and sacrificial animal) and "female genitals" (specifically the hairless
    genitals of young girls). Unfortunately, the American slang usages "pork" and
    "meat" are unavailable for translation, since they refer to the penis. I have therefore
    decided to use "pussy" even though the jokes about hairiness and about cooking
    and eating pork do not quite fit it (the Greeks did not eat cats).
747 "at the Mysteries": initiates at the Eleusinian Mysteries (47 n.) brought pigs with them
    to sacrifice at the preliminary ceremonies.
751-2 The Megarian makes a grim joke about his country's miserable poverty; Dicaeopolis
    hears (or feigns to have heard) "drink" so that his pleasantry is inappropriate.

Dicaeopolis
What else at Megara? How's the price of grain?

Megarian
As high as it can get, just like the gods.

Dicaeopolis
So what've you got, some salt?

Megarian
                    Don't you control it?   760

Dicaeopolis
Some garlic?

Megarian
            Garlic? Every time you guys
invade our country, you're like a horde of mice,
you dig up all the garlic bulbs with hoes.

Dicaeopolis
What have you got?

Megarian
            I got some grade-A pussies.

Dicaeopolis
All right! Let's see them.

Megarian
                    You're gonna like this fine.   765
Go on and cop a feel. They're nice and soft.

Dicaeopolis
What's this supposed to be?

Megarian
                    I told you: pussies.

Dicaeopolis
Explain your meaning. Where's this from?

Megarian
                              From Megara.
You say it ain't no pussy?

Dicaeopolis
                    Doesn't look it.

Megarian
Well I'll be damned. Look, this guy don't trust nothin'.   770
He says this ain't no pussy. I tell you what.
You want, I'll bet you a pound of seasoned salt
that this here's pussy in the broad sense of the word.

Dicaeopolis
All right, but it's a human being's!

Megarian
> Sure,
belongs to me. Whose else you think it is?   775
You wanna hear it squeal?

Dicaeopolis
> Why certainly
I would.

Megarian
OK now, pussy, make a sound.
You won't? You're clamming up, you goddamned girl?
I swear to God I'll take you home again!

Girl
> Meow meow!

Megarian
That ain't no pussy?

Dicaeopolis
> Looks like pussy now,
but all grown up it's a beaver.

Megarian
> In five years,
I tell you, it'll be just like its momma.

Dicaeopolis
But I can't even cook and eat it.

Megarian
> No?   785
What's to stop you?

Dicaeopolis
> Hasn't got the meat.

Megarian
Too young. But when it fleshes out a bit
it'll get the meat that's pink and long and hard.
And if you wanna rear one, here's another.

Dicaeopolis
Its pussy looks just like the other one's!

Megarian
Why sure: it's got the selfsame mom and dad.   790
And when it fattens up and grows some hair,
it'll be a nice pussy to offer up to Venus.

Dicaeopolis
But pussies don't get offered up to Venus.°

Megarian
So pussy ain't for Venus? Who else then?
And look, the flesh of these here pussies is   795
delicious when it's skewered on a spit.

Dicaeopolis
So tell me, can they suck without their mother?

Megarian
Hell yes. They'll suck without their father, too.

Dicaeopolis
And what do they like to suck on?

Megarian
                              Anything.
Ask 'em yourself.

Dicaeopolis
                    Here pussy.

Girl A
                              Meow meow!   800

Dicaeopolis
Would you like to gnaw this hambone?°

Girl A
                              Meow meow.

Dicaeopolis
Then how about a lollipop?°

Girl A
                         Meow meow!

Dicaeopolis
And how about you? Want one?

Girl B
                              Meow meow!

Dicaeopolis
They mew so loud when I say lollipops!
Go inside, someone, get some lollipops   805

---

793 At Athens Aphrodite (Roman Venus), the goddess of sexual enjoyment, did not re-
     ceive pigs in sacrifice, reputedly because her lover Adonis had been killed by a boar.
801 "Hambone" translates "chickpeas," Athenian slang for penis.
802 "dried Phibalian figs," a favorite childrens' sweet.

for the pussies. Will they eat them? Oh my god,
just look at them get down! Dear Heracles!
Where are these pussies from? From Hungary?°

Megarian
They didn't gobble all the lollipops.
I managed to snag this lolly for myself.   810

Dicaeopolis
By god, a real delightful pair of pets.
How much will the pussies cost me? Name your price.

Megarian
I'll give you this one here for a bunch of garlic;
the other one, you want her, a pound of salt.

Dicaeopolis
I'll take them. Just a moment, please.

Megarian
                                        All right!   815
O God of Traders, may I sell my wife
at such a price, and my dear mother, too!

Informer
Your identity, sir.

Megarian
                    Megarian pussy-seller.

Informer°
Then I denounce these cats as contraband
and you as well!

Megarian
                    Ah, here we go again!   820
We're back to where our troubles first began.

Informer
No Megarian backtalk! Let me have the sack!

Megarian
Dicaeopolis! Dicaeopolis! I'm denounced!

Dicaeopolis
By whom? Denounced by whom? Commissioners,°
aren't you supposed to keep informers out?   825

---

808 "from Tragasae," a city in Asia Minor, punning on *tragein*, "eat."
818 For informers see 519 n.
824 He refers to his straps (723-4).

And you: you're pecking around without a pecker.°

Informer
I'm not to denounce the enemy?

Dicaeopolis
                          You'll regret it,
unless you do your informing somewhere else.

Megarian
What a plague they are in Athens, these informers!

Dicaeopolis
Don't fret, Megarian. Here's the price you asked   830
for the pussies. Take the garlic and the salt,
and best of luck.

Megarian
                          Luck's alien to my land.

Dicaeopolis
Is luck forbidden? If so I'll take the blame.

Megarian
Farewell, my pussies. Even without me try
to get jelly with the roll a man may give you.°   835

                          Chorus

Chorus (6)°
This man at least is truly blest!
    You've seen his plan mature.
Just sitting in his market-place
    he'll rake it in for sure.

And should some Ctesias appear°
    or other stoolie clown,   840
he'll scream and cry in agony
    whenever he sits down.

No man will aggravate you here
    and cut into the queue,
no fag will bring his cooties here

---

826 "Why do you suppose you can shed light on anything without a lamp-wick?" The joke
      is best explained on the assumption that "wick" here means "penis": perhaps the
      Informer does not wear a phallos, which would mark him as unmanly.
835 The Megarian departs and Dicaeopolis takes the girls inside.
836 After the parabasis (626 n.) it was normal for the Chorus, between episodes, to abuse
      individual spectators.
839 Ctesias is otherwise unknown, but the name ('Grasper') is appropriate.

and rub them off on you.°

You'll jostle no Cleonymus°
and have to wash your shirt;   845
you'll never bump Hyperbolus°
and touch his legal dirt.

Cratinus won't walk up to you,°
old fart with blow-dried curls,
as if that makes him look to be
a hand with married girls.

This Model T of poetry
composes in first gear,   850
and his exhaust-pipe smells so bad
you'd think a skunk's in there.

Nor yet will vile Pauson come°
to mock you to your face,
nor yet again Lysistratus,°
the same of all his race,

a man so deep in misery,   855
so hungry and so bleak,
he goes without a decent meal
eight days in every week.

EPISODE II

*(Theban, Dicaeopolis, Nicarchus, Theban's Slave, Pipers, Dicaeopolis' Slaves
and Children)*

Theban°
By Heracles, my hump is really tired!

---

843 They mention Prepis, perhaps the man who a few years later served as Council Secretary.
844 See 89 n.
846 Hyperbolus, whose wealth was associated with lamp-making, was at this time a notorious prosecutor and an ambitious popular politician in the mold of Cleon, whose position as leading "demagogue" he in fact assumed after Cleon's death in 422.
848 Cratinus had been the leading comic poet in the generation before Aristophanes and a pioneer in the creation of political comedy. At this time he was elderly (he died some three years later), but he was still composing and therefore a rival; indeed he was to win his last victory in 423, over Aristophanes's *Clouds*.
853 Pauson was an impoverished painter known for caricatures, jokes and riddles.
854 There were several men named Lysistratus in this period; this one seems to be the man ridiculed in Aristophanes's *Wasps* as a practical joker.
860 Like the Megarian earlier, this Theban speaks in his local dialect. Boeotia (often bracketed with Sparta as Athens' chief enemy) was, unlike Megara, a rich and fertile region.

Now very carefully, slave, put down the lettuce.
You pipers that have made the trek from Thebes,
pick up your pipes and play "The Dog's Asshole."°

Dicaeopolis

Stop, damn you! Go away, you bumblebees!
From where did all these cursed buzzers come,   865
these sons of Chaeris, flying to my door?°

Theban

By Heracles' nephew, friend, I owe you one.
They've followed me blowing all the way from Thebes;
they've blown the leaves right off my lettuces.
But maybe you'd like to buy some goods from me?   870
I've got some game with two wings, some with four.°

Dicaeopolis

My greetings, dear Boeotian, eater of spam.°
What have you?

Theban

           All the goods Boeotia boasts.
Got marjoram, pennyroyal, rush-mats, wicks for lamps,
got ducks and jackdaws, francolins and coots,   875
got wrens and grebes—

Dicaeopolis

              You've hit my market-place
just like an autumn storm with its fowl winds.

Theban

Got geese, got rabbits, got some foxes too,
got moles and hedgehogs, kitty-cats and badgers,
got martens, otters, eels from Lake Copais—°   880

Dicaeopolis

The most delectable morsel known to man?
If you've got eels, please introduce me to them!

Theban

Most venerable leader of these Copaic nymphs,
step forth from your sack and greet the gentleman.

---

863 The song in question, otherwise unknown, suggests rusticity and/or vulgarity.
866 See 16 n.
871 "four-winged" (a surprise for "four-footed") refers to locusts (a poor food).
872 "spam" translates *kollix*, a kind of rough barley bread.
880 Copaic eels were a Boeotian delicacy much prized at Athens and used by Aristophanes elsewhere to exemplify the war's deprivations. Suitably to the moment, lines 881-94 parody tragic scenes of reunion.

Dicaeopolis

O dearest one and long my heart's desire,   885
you've come, the fondest of wish of comic dancers
and dear to Morychus! Attendants, bring me out°
a barbecue grill and something to fan it with.
Behold, my children, this noblest eel just come
in answer to our prayers of six long years.   890
Address her nicely, kids, and in her honor
I'll give you a gift of nice charcoal briquets.°
But take her hence, for never death itself
shall part me from her or her sauce tartare!

Theban

There's still the little matter of my payment.   895

Dicaeopolis

I thought you'd give me that as market-tax.
What else did you say you want to sell to me?

Theban

It's all for sale.

Dicaeopolis

        Well, how much for the lot?
Or take some goods from here back home?

Theban

                  A swap?
Hmm, something from Athens that's not found in Boeotia.   900

Dicaeopolis

Your smartest buy would be Phalerian sprats,
or pottery.

Theban

      Sprats or pots? We've got 'em there.
No, something you've got lots of but we've got none.

Dicaeopolis

I've got it. Why not take back an informer?
I'll pack him like a pot.

Theban

           By the Twain Gods,   905
I'd make a handsome sum importing one,
one like a little monkey full of tricks.

---

887 Morychus was a noted lover of fine food.
892 Dicaeopolis apparently teases his children: instead of a real gift, they will get to set up
    the grill.

Dicaeopolis
And look! Nicharchus on his way to snitch!°

Theban
He's very small.

Dicaeopolis
                    But not an ounce of quality.

Nicarchus
Whose packages are these?

Theban
                         Belong to me,   910
by god, from Thebes.

Nicarchus
                In that case I, in person,
denounce them as contraband.

Theban
                      What's wrong with you,
declaring war and battle on my birdies?

Nicarchus
And I denounce you, too.

Theban
                 For doing what?

Nicarchus
I'll tell you, for the audience's benefit.   915
From enemy territory you've imported lamp-wicks.

Dicaeopolis
You mean you'd turn him in because of wicks?

Nicarchus
A man could torch the dockyard with this wick.

Dicaeopolis
The dockyard with a wick?

Nicarchus
               That's right.

Dicaeopolis
                     And how?

Nicarchus
A Theban ties the wick to a beetle's back,   920

---

908 Otherwise unknown.

then lights it up and sends it to the docks
in a drain as soon as the north wind starts to blow.
The fire, once it started among the ships,
would quickly blaze.

Dicaeopolis
            You wretched idiot!
A blaze begun by a beetle and a wick.   925

Nicarchus
A witness!

Dicaeopolis
            Grab him, stuff something in his mouth.
Give me some sawdust, so I can pack him up
like a pot, so he won't be damaged during shipment.

LYRIC SCENE IV

Chorus Leader
Dear fellow, please take care
   as you get the parcel packed;   930
we want our foreign friend
   to bring it home intact.

Dicaeopolis
Don't worry! For, you know,
   it makes a special sound,
a babble, fire-cracked,
   for loathesomeness renowned.

Chorus Leader
Whatever use could it be to him?   935

Dicaeopolis
A vessel for every use!
A mixing-bowl for evil,
a mortar for lawsuits,
a lamp to expose officials,
a shaker to stir up trouble.

Chorus Leader
But wouldn't you be scared   940
   to put among your toys
a vessel such as this,
   that's always making noise?

Dicaeopolis
It's very strong, dear sir,
so even if I chose,
I'd never break it, though

I hang it by the toes.   945
Chorus Leader
You're set now, Theban!
Theban
Can't wait to use it!
Chorus Leader
Now then, dear Theban, use
this man as you see fit;
take him and sic him on
whatever foe you like: 950
an informer for every use!
Dicaeopolis
It wasn't easy packing the bastard up.
You may load your pot now, Theban, and take it home.
Theban
You there, my slaveling, put your shoulder to it.
Dicaeopolis
Make sure you're very careful carrying it,   955
although it's pretty rotten merchandise.
If you make a handsome profit on this shipment,
you won't run out of informers to import.°

EPISODE III
(Dicaeopolis, Lamachus' Slave)

Slave
Dicaeopolis!
Dicaeopolis
                    Why all this yelling?
Slave
                    Why?
Lamachus gave me a drachma to pay you   960
to buy some thrushes for the Pitcher Feast,°

---

958 The Thebans leave, and Dicaeopolis is on his way inside with their goods when Lama-
    chus' slave approaches on the run.
961 The Pitcher Feast (*Khoes*) was celebrated on the second day (of three) of the Anthesteria,
    a great mid-winter festival (around February) honoring Dionysus. The pitcher
    in question (the *khous*) held about three quarts. Among the many religious and
    carnivalesque activities that took place on this day (and are reproduced by Di-
    caeopolis) were drinking contests and a state banquet to which guests were invited
    by the Priest of Dionysus. Also relevant to our play, with its hymeneal ending, was
    the Sacred Marriage between the wife of the King Archon, the official in charge of
    the state religion, and Dionysus (perhaps on this occasion impersonated by the King
    Archon himself).

and three more drachmas for a Copaic eel.°

Dicaeopolis
Which Lamachus is this who seeks the eel?

Slave
The awesome, strong-armed Gorgon-brandisher
who shakes a triple shadow-casting crest!   965

Dicaeopolis
No deal, by god, not even for his shield!
He can shake his triple crest at the hotdog stand.
He makes a fuss, I'll call the commissioners.°
I'll take this load of goodies for myself,
and fly inside on thrush and blackbird wings.°   970

Chorus

Chorus (7¹)
O city, do you see how smart
    this man is, and how wise,
how making peace enables him
    to sell fine merchandise?
His store includes not only things
    for use around the home,
but also things most fittingly   975
    consumed when they're well-done.

Chorus Leader
With ease does he acquire whatever's fine and good.
We'll never ask the War-god to visit our neighborhood,
nor in his presence sing a patriotic tune,°   980
for when the War-god drinks he acts the perfect goon.
When we were very prosperous he burst upon the scene,
committed crimes, upended and wasted everything.
He'd fight and when we said, "sit down and have a sip;
let's drink a friendly toast to our good fellowship,"   985
instead he'd turn more violent, set fire to our vines,
and tramp them till he'd squeezed out every drop of wine.

---

962 See 880 n.
968 See 824 n.
970 The phrase parodies a lyric poem otherwise unattested. Dicaeopolis goes inside.
980 The "Harmodius Song," a traditional patriotic drinking song that celebrated Harmo-
    dius and his friend Aristogeiton, who in 514 assassinated Hipparchus, brother of the
    last Athenian tyrant, Hippias. Several versions of the song are preserved.

Chorus (7²)
> To dinner he's prepared to fly,
>> his pride is very great;
> to flaunt his feasting he has tossed
>> these feathers from his gate.

> Of lovely Aphrodite and
>> the Graces her relations
> we call upon the foster-child
>> sweet Reconciliation.°

Chorus Leader
> How fair a face you had I never understood!   990
> I wish that Cupid might unite us two for good,
> that Cupid in the painting with flowers in his hat,
> unless perchance you think me too antique for that.
> But should we grapple I'd still put you down three times.°
> I'd first shove in a long hard row of tender vines,°   995
> and then alongside that I'd lay some fresh fig-shoots
> and finally some grapes—would I, the ancient coot!—
> and all around the plot a stand of olive-trees,
> so we could oil ourselves for every New Moon Feast.°

LYRIC SCENE V
(Herald, Dicaeopolis, Chorus, Dercetes, Best Man, Maid of Honor)

Herald
> Hear this! As custom has it, drink your pitchers   1000
> at the trumpet call. The man who drinks up first
> will win a wine-skin the size of Ctesiphon's!°

Dicaeopolis
> You slaves, you women, aren't you listening?
> What are you doing? Don't you hear the Herald?
> Now braise and roast and turn and then unskewer   1005
> the rabbits, quickly; string the garlands, too.
> Bring me the spits, so I can fix the thrushes.

---

989 The same personification is actually brought on stage, in the form of a naked girl, in
  Aristophanes's peace-play *Lysistrata*, produced in 411.
994 The ability to copulate three times in succession was a proverbial proof of virility.
995 In these lines, which celebrate the farmer's return to his fields and vineyards as a
  result of "reconciliation," the agricultural language is, by metaphor, simultaneously
  understood as sexual activity with "Reconciliation," personified as a young girl.
999 Each month at the new moon people had festive dinners, to which participants would
  come bathed and anointed with fragrant oil.
1002 Evidently Ctesiphon (otherwise unknown) had a "beer belly" of impressive size.
  The *ekkyklema* (408 n.) is rolled out; on it are Dicaeopolis, some slaves, food, cooking
  utensils and a lighted brazier.

Chorus (8¹)
> I envy you your plan so shrewd,
> or rather this delicious food,
> sir, here before us now.   1010

Dicaeopolis
> Just wait until you have a look
> at the thrushes being cooked!

Chorus
> I think you're quite correct again.

Dicaeopolis
> Start poking up the flame.

Chorus
> You hear how master chef-ily,   1015
> how subtly, how gourmettily
> he does the job himself?

Dercetes
> Oh dear, what sadness!

Dicaeopolis
>   Heracles! who's this?

Dercetes
> A man with sorrows.

Dicaeopolis
>   Keep them to yourself.

Dercetes
> Dear sir, since you alone possess a treaty,   1020
> give me some peace, if only five years' worth.

Dicaeopolis
> What's wrong?

Dercetes
>   I've lost my oxen; now I'm ruined!

Dicaeopolis
> Lost where?

Dercetes
>   Boeotians plundered them at Phyle.°

Dicaeopolis
> Thrice wretched man! And you're still wearing white?

1023 An Attic deme on Mt. Parnes (348 n.) near the Boeotian frontier.

Dercetes
>And that, my god, when those oxen had kept
>me rolling in manure!   1025

Dicaeopolis
>>So what do you want?

Dercetes
>I've ruined my eyes with weeping for my oxen.
>If you care at all about Dercetes of Phyle,
>put some of your peace in both my eyes right now.

Dicaeopolis
>But, foolish man, I'm not a public doctor.   1030

Dercetes
>Go on, I beg you, so I can find my oxen!

Dicaeopolis
>No way. Go take your tears to Medicare.°

Dercetes
>Oh please, just drip me one small drop of peace
>into this fennel-stalk I've got with me.

Dicaeopolis
>Not even a teeny drop. Cry somewhere else!   1035

Dercetes
>Poor me, poor little beasts of burden lost!°

Chorus (8²)
>The man's discovered something rare
>in his treaty, but he wants to share
>>with no one, it would seem.

Dicaeopolis
>Pour honey on the sausages,   1040
>>and brown the cuttlefish!

Chorus
>You hear his loud commanding peals?

Dicaeopolis
>It's time to broil the eels!

Chorus
>I'll die of hunger from the smell
>and from your words, my friends as well,   1045

1032 "to Pittalus' clinic;" a public doctor mentioned again in this play (1222) and else-
>where.
1036 Dercetes goes away wailing.

if you keep shouting thus.

Dicaeopolis
Now roast these till they're delicately browned.

Best Man
Dicaeopolis!

Dicaeopolis
Who's this that's calling me?

Best Man
A bridegroom sends this piece of meat to you
from the wedding-feast.

Dicaeopolis
                He's nice, whoever he is.   1050

Best Man
And he asks you, in return for the piece of meat,
to pour a cup of peace into this flask,
so instead of fighting he can stay home fucking.

Dicaeopolis
Away with the meat, away, don't give it to me!
I wouldn't pour you any for a million bucks.   1055
But who's this girl?

Best Man
             The maid of honor, with
a secret message for you from the bride.

Dicaeopolis
Come, what have you got to say? My god, how funny
this request is from he bride! She asks me, please
arrange for her husband's cock to stay at home.°   1060
Bring me the treaty; with her alone I'll share:
as a woman she's not responsible for the war.
Now hold the flask up here, this way, my girl.
You know how this is used? You tell the bride:
whenever they call up troops, take some of this   1065
and rub it on your husband's cock at night.°
Now take away the treaty. Where's my ladle?
I want to decant my wine for the Pitcher Feast.

1060 In actual life a maid of honor would probably not have used the obscene word Dicaeopolis reports her as using.
1066 The best man and maid of honor leave.

EPISODE IV

(Chorus Leader, Messengers I and II, Lamachus, Dicaeopolis, Dicaeopolis'
Slave, Lamachus' Slave)

Chorus Leader
But look, here comes a man with furrowed brows,
in a hurry, as if he brings some dire news.   1070

Messenger I
Dear me! Oh hardships, battles, Lamachuses!°

Lamachus
Who makes such racket round my bronze-bossed halls?

Messenger I
The generals command you leave today
and quickly, with your crests and your platoons,
to guard the winter passes in the snow.   1075
They're informed that, on the Pot and Pitcher Feasts,
Boeotian bandits plan a plunder-raid.

Lamachus
Oh generals more numerous than smart!
How awful that I can't attend the Feast.

Dicaeopolis
Hooray for the Lamachean expedition!   1080

Lamachus
Alas and damn, would you now mock at me?

Dicaeopolis
You want to fight, you four-feathered Godzilla?°

Lamachus
Ah me!
What an order this messenger messages to me!

Dicaeopolis
Ah me! What's my message from this second runner?

Messenger II
Dicaeopolis!

Dicaeopolis
            Yes?

1071 The Messenger runs up to Lamachus' door.
1082 Comparing Lamachus to the hideous monster Geryon, who was robbed and killed by
   (the Boeotian native) Heracles, and giving him an epithet suggesting insects (traditionally Geryon was triple-bodied).

Messenger II
To dinner on the double;   1085
march. Bring your picnic basket and your Pitcher.
The Priest of Dionysus summons you.°
But hurry: you've held up dinner far too long.
Except for you, all's set and ready to go:
the couches, tables, pillows, rugs and blankets,   1090
the garlands, perfume, hors-d'oeuvres, prostitutes,
the cakes, the pastries, sesame-crackers, rolls,
the dancing-girls who'll pipe the anthem—cute!
Come on and hurry up!

Lamachus
Oh woe is me!
[Can flesh endure such grievous deprivation?]°

Dicaeopolis
Well, blame your patron, that big Gorgon there.°   1095
Lock up the house and pack my dinner, boy.

Lamachus
Boy, fetch my mess-kit and bring it here to me.

Dicaeopolis
Boy, fetch my basket and bring it here to me.

Lamachus
My K-ration, boy, my flavored salt and onions.

Dicaeopolis
The salmon-steaks, no onion: I'm tired of that.°   1100

Lamachus
Bring me some hard salt-fish, boy, wrapped in leaves.

Dicaeopolis
Bring me a juicy steak; I'll cook it there.

Lamachus
Bring me here the twin plumes from my helmet.

Dicaeopolis
Bring me here the pigeons and the thrushes.

Lamachus
So fair and gleaming is the ostrich-plume!   1105

1087 See 961 n.
1094 Alan Sommerstein's suggestion for the lost line that must (because of the wording of
    line 1096) have originally stood here.
1095 Perhaps a cue to withdraw the *ekkyklema* (1002 n.; compare 479).
1100 Onions were staple field-rations.

Dicaeopolis
So fair and lovely brown the pigeon-meat!

Lamachus
Old fellow, cease your laughter at my equipment.

Dicaeopolis
Old fellow, cease your leering at my thrushes.

Lamachus
Bring out my crest-case and my triple crests.

Dicaeopolis
Bring out my casserole and my rabbit stew.   1110

Lamachus
What's this? Have moths been eating up my crests?

Dicaeopolis
What's this? Must I eat the rabbit before dinner?

Lamachus
Old fellow, please refrain from addressing me.

Dicaeopolis
Not you; you see, my slave and I are arguing.
You want to bet, boy, with Lamachus as judge,   1115
which makes the better eating, locust or thrush?

Lamachus
Oh! What impudence!

Dicaeopolis
                    He's strongly for the locusts.

Lamachus
Boy, boy, take down my spear and bring it hither.

Dicaeopolis
Boy, boy, take off the sausage and bring it here.

Lamachus
Come, let me draw the spear-case off my weapon.   1120
Here, hold on, boy.

Dicaeopolis
                    Boy, hold the skewer firmly.

Lamachus
Hand me the staves, boy, that support my shield.

Dicaeopolis
Hand me the loaves, boy, that support my belly.

Lamachus
Hand hither my buckler round and Gorgon-faced.°

Dicaeopolis
Give me a pizza round and cheesy-faced.°   1125

Lamachus
Is not this insolence plain in the eyes of men?

Dicaeopolis
Isn't this great pizza in the eyes of men?

Lamachus
Pour on the oil, boy, for in this bronze
I see an old man indictable for cowardice.

Dicaeopolis
Pour honey; for in the cake an old man appears   1130
telling Lamachus, son of Gorgon, to go to hell.

Lamachus
Hand hither, boy, my warlike coat of mail.

Dicaeopolis
Hand over, boy, my drinklike party-suit.

Lamachus
In this I bolster me to meet the foe.

Dicaeopolis
In this I bolster me to meet the drinkers.   1135

Lamachus
My sleeping-bag fasten, boy, upon the shield.

Dicaeopolis
My dinner fasten, boy, upon the basket.

Lamachus
And I shall porter the mess-kit by myself.

Dicaeopolis
And I will take my coat and be running off.

Lamachus
Enclasp and raise the shield, boy, and be off.   1140
It snows, brr brr, we're in for serious weather.

Dicaeopolis
Pick up the dinner, we're off to serious drinking.°

1124 see 574 n.
1125 The *plakous* (flat-cake), when topped with cheese, was indeed pizza-like.
1142 Lamachus exits to one side of the stage, Dicaeopolis to the other.

Chorus Leader
>Fare well on your expeditions!
>How different your conditions!
>*He'll* wear a crown and drink at ease;　　　　1145
>*you'll* stand your lonely watch and freeze,
>while he has a whirl
>with a fresh young girl
>and gets his weenie squeezed.

Chorus (9¹)
>Antimachus the bureaucrat,　　　　1150
>　composer of bad verse,
>who spits while talking, may the Lord
>　destroy, as he deserves.
>For as sponsor of a comedy
>　in this Lenaean show,°
>at banquet-time he told us all
>　to pack our things and go!　　　　1155
>I want to live to see the day
>　when squid is what he craves,
>and there it is, well cooked and hot,
>　come safely through the waves
>and making port at tableside,
>　and as he fills his tray,
>I pray a dog will snap it up　　　　1160
>　and carry it away!

Chorus (9²)
>That's one misfortune on his head;
>　and here's another curse:
>one night, as he walks home alone
>　from riding on his horse,　　　　1165
>encountering some drunken lout
>　who wants to break his bones
>(the lunatic Orestes!), may°
>　he fumble for a stone,
>but in the darkness may he put
>　within his groping mitt
>a piece of hot manure that

1154 Producers were expected to hold a banquet for the troupe after the competition was over (see Introduction); Antimachus' behavior on the occasion recalled here, otherwise undocumented, was perhaps motivated by the failure of his troupe to win.

1168 Orestes (a nickname recalling the mythic son of Agememnon, who wandered insane to Athens after killing his own mother) is mentioned elsewhere in comedy as a notorious mugger.

somebody freshly shit,   1170
and may he rush upon his foe
   with missile held aloft,
and may he miss his shot and hit
   Cratinus in the chops!°

EXODOS

(Messenger III, Lamachus, Dicaeopolis, Dancing Girls)

Messenger III
Ye vassals of the House of Lamachus,
heat water, heat some water in a basin,   1175
prepare lint padding, ready liniments,
some greasy wool, a bandage for his ankle!
He's been wounded, jumping o'er a ditch, by a stake,
his ankle's twisted back and out of joint,
and, falling on a stone, he's cracked his head   1180
and waked the sleeping gorgon from her shield!
When he saw his valiant boastard-feather fall
upon the rocks, he howled this awful cry,
"O brilliant visage, ne'er I'll see you more;
I leave thee, light of mine; I am undone!"   1185
Thus having spoken, and falling in the ditch,
he rose and faced his men in panic flight
and chased and routed bandits with his spear.
And here he is himself! Open the gates!

Lamachus
Ah me! Ah me!   1190
Hateful as hell
   my bloody pains, oh woe!
I am no more,
   by foeman's spear struck down!
But that would truly be an agony   1195
if Dicaeopolis laughed at my bad luck!

Dicaeopolis
Ah me! Ah me!
What gorgeous tits,
   as firm as little quinces!
Tenderly kiss me,
   my little golden jewels!   1200
One suck my lips, the other plunge your tongue,

1173 See 848 n. Might Antimachus' chorus have been performers in a play by Cratinus?

for I'm the first to drain my pitcher dry!

Lamachus
O direful conjunction of my woes!
Oh, oh, the agony of my injuries!   1205

Dicaeopolis
Hey, hey, hello there, Lamachus m'lord!

Lamachus
Hateful am I, cursed am I!

Dicaeopolis
Kissing again? Biting again?

Lamachus
Wretched me! Grievous cost!

Dicaeopolis
You mean they made you pay for the Pitcher Feast?°

Lamachus
Apollo Healer, Healer!

Dicaeopolis
But we're not feasting for Apollo now.

Lamachus
Take hold of my leg, take hold. Ouch ouch!
Hold tightly, comrades mine!   1215

Dicaeopolis
Take hold of my cock, both hold the middle!°
Hold tightly, darlings mine!

Lamachus
I'm dizzy, I feel that rock on my head,
I swoon as night comes on!

Dicaeopolis
I'm sleepy, I feel a rock in my pants,   1220
I'll fuck as night comes on!

Lamachus
Take me away to the hospital,°
with gentle healing hands!

1211 Probably the usual custom that guests equally share the cost of a banquet was not
    observed at the Pitcher Feast; likely another dig at Lamachus' poverty as well.
1216 They grab his phallos (see Introduction).
1222 See 1032 n.

Dicaeopolis
Take me away to the judges and King;°
I want my wine-skin prize! 1225

Lamachus
A lance most woeful's pierced me to the bone!

Dicaeopolis
My pitcher's empty: hail the champion!

Chorus Leader
As you like, old man, we hail the champion!

Dicaeopolis
What's more, my wine was neat and gulped straight down.

Chorus Leader
Hooray then, noble hero, and take your wine-skin! 1230

Dicaeopolis
Then follow me and sing "All Hail the Champion"!

Chorus (10)
We will follow
for your sake,
singing 'All Hail'
in your wake,
for you and for
your wine-skin!

1224 The King Archon (961 n.).